The Treasures of Galveston Bay

The Treasures of Galveston Bay

Facts and legends of hidden, lost, and buried treasures located in the Galveston Bay area.

By Carroll Lewis

TEXIAN PRESS • 1977 • WACO

First Edition Printed 1-3-1966
First Revised Edition Printed 11-30-1977
Second Revised Edition Printed 6-30-1980
Third Revised Edition Printed 5-1-1991
Fourth Revised Edition Printed 6-1-1992
Fifth Revised Edition Printed 7-1-2002

Library of Congress Catalog Card No. 66-21556

ISBN 0-87244-052-4

Published by

Dedicated to all those who enjoy glimpses of the past while searching for the lost treasures of history.

Foreword

The company of treasure hunters is a large one. It includes such notables as Francis Drake, Walter Raleigh, Winston Churchill, George Washington, Franklin Delano Roosevelt and John Fitzgerald Kennedy.

One of the earliest and most successful treasure hunters was Sir William Phips, who, in 1687, found and recovered over $1,000,000 from the wreck of a Spanish galleon sunk on the Bahama Silver Shoals. For this he was knighted by King James II and made Governor of the Massachusetts Colony.

This spirit of adventure and romanticism has attracted countless of others to the fascinating intrigue of treasure hunting. There are treasures buried all over the world; so no one lacks a place to look.

In the Caribbean, there are many islands that would quicken the imagination of one such as Robert Louis Stevenson to thrill and entertain us with his *Treasure Island*, but for sheer treasure trove, there is none so prolific and exciting as the island of Galveston and its adjoining bays.

The magnificent Nineteenth Century Victorian homes in the City of Galveston are treasures enough to behold, but the legends and treasure tales that abound about this area would make Long John Silver turn green with envy. So shoulder your shovel, take this book in hand, and come along with me to discover some of the treasures of Galveston Bay.

Carroll Lewis

Preface

The rapid and accelerating growth of museums, both in this country and abroad, is evidence that people everywhere are suddenly becoming aware of the importance of their heritage. Most of these new museums are in the smaller cities, and they have as one of their principal objectives the collection and study of historical artifacts from their own locality. It is fortunate that these regional museums are being developed, because the objects of their study are rapidly being lost or destroyed.

Before a museum can become an effective force in its community, it must have an audience which supports its activities and is interested in what it is doing. The Houston Museum of Natural Science has recently assisted in the formation of three of these new museums in the Big Thicket, Brazosport, and the Alabama-Coushatta Indian Reservation. In each of these museums emphasis has been placed on the early history of the area, for this is a certain way to gain local support.

In each of these new museums there are devoted workers who are designing the exhibits and developing collections of interesting objects to display. Here as in all museums, however, the controlling factors for growth are often finances and publicity. I can think of no surer way for any museum to succeed than to discover a horde of Spanish gold or perhaps the treasure of Jean Lafitte.

I am sure that not everyone who reads Carroll Lewis' book will find these treasures, and perhaps no one will. I am also sure that no one who reads this book will be the poorer for it. There is treasure in knowledge, as well as in silver and gold, and Mr. Lewis has assembled more information about the early history of Galveston Bay than is available in any other single source. His material was not gathered solely from the archives of libraries but from actual research "in the field"—interviewing old timers, poking around cemeteries, comparing existing shorelines with old maps, and performing the myriad tasks necessary to cross-check such information.

The history of Texas has been inextricably associated with the Galveston area since Cabeza de Vaca was shipwrecked there in 1528. The Island and the Bay have witnessed the Spanish conquest, the invasion by the French, the somnolence of Mexican colonialism disturbed by settlers from the North, the Texas Revolution, days of the Republic, entry into the Union, secession and the dark days of the Civil War and Reconstruction, and finally the rapid period of growth as the Nineteenth Century gave way to the Twentieth. During all this time a certain amount of gold and silver has been finding its way, either by accident or design, into Galveston sands or its murky waters.

But gold and silver are not the only treasures of Galveston Bay, although they may be the most powerful lure that draws us toward the past. The treasure seekers that I have known have all learned quickly that if gold is not to be found, a square iron nail or a hand-blown bottle can become an important part in the treasure of our heritage.

I am sure that the reader will find the information revealed in this book a most interesting foundation toward the enjoyment of these treasures.

By Thomas E. Pulley, PhD., 1957-1985
Director Emeritus of the Houston Museum of Natural Science

The "Piece of Eight" that appears on the title page of this book was drawn by Bob Abernathy of Waco, Texas. It was sketched from an original found by the author's son, Carroll A. Lewis, III, near the mouth of Clear Creek in June of 1965.

Contents

Illustrations

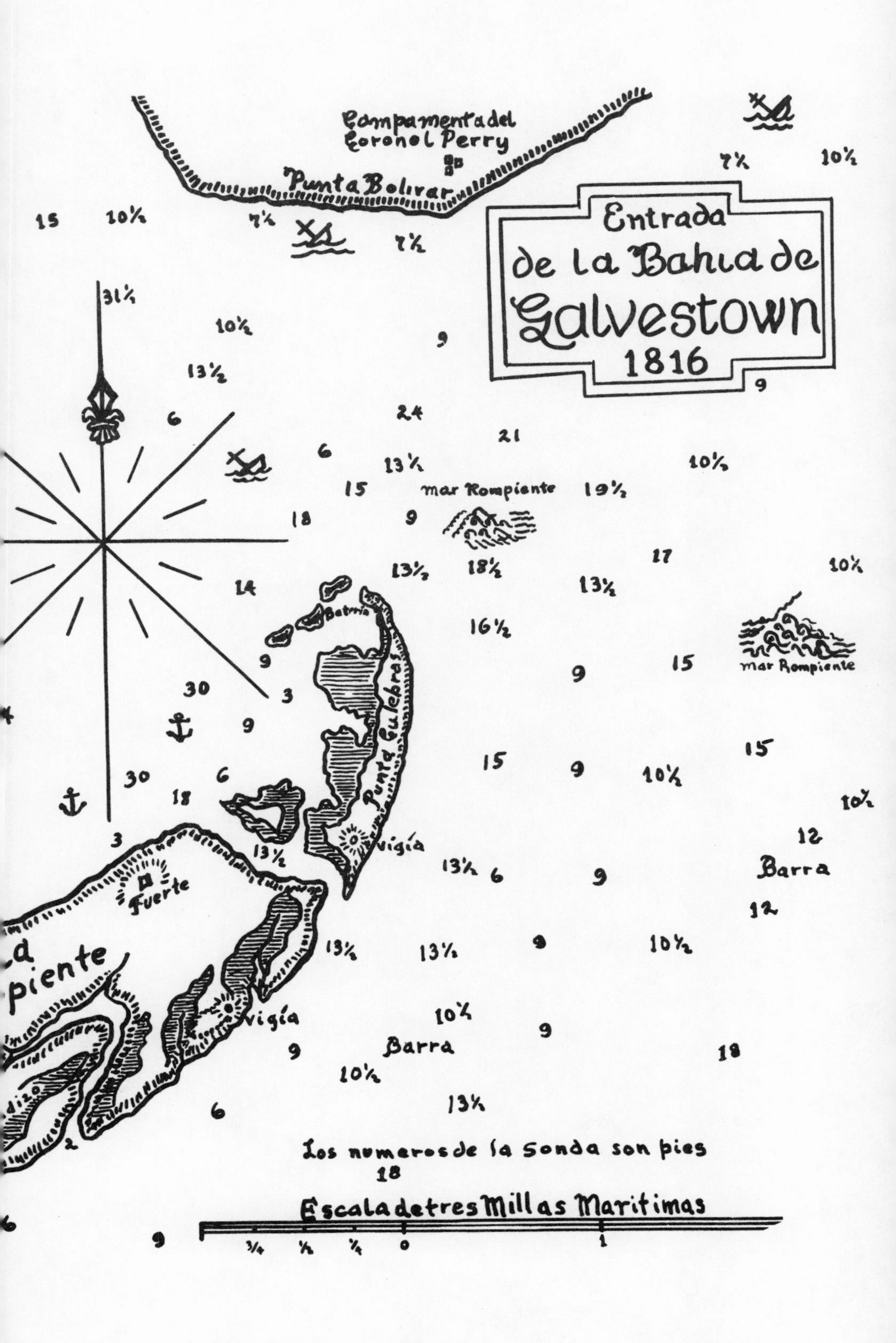
Entrada
de la Bahia de
Galvestown
1816
Campamenta del
Coronel Perry
Punta Bolivar
mar Rompiente
mar Rompiente
Batria
Punta Culebras
Vigía
Fuerte
Vigía
Barra
Barra
Los numeros de la Sonda son pies
Escala de tres Millas Maritimas
3/4
1/2
1/4
0
1

Chapter One

Treasure From the Gulf

There are more different treasures to be found around the vicinity of Galveston Bay than in any other comparable area in the world!

Here, one may find artifacts from vanished Indian civilizations; relics left by the Spanish conquistadors; cargoes of sunken ships; valuables hidden by early pioneers; caches of gold and silver buried by invading armies; vestiges of forgotten ghost towns; antiquities from the Napoleonic Wars, Spanish Liberation, American and Texas Revolutions, and the Civil War.

Not to be overlooked, there are also many natural treasures to be found: The sunny beaches with their seashells, birds, sand and surf; the waters—considered by international racing contestants as the best sailing in the world; the waterfowl and fish that abound for sport and palate; plus the mild climate that pervades over all.

And, of course, pirate treasure. In *Jean Lafitte, Gentleman Rover*, Stanley Clisby Arthur observed: "Countless are the legends clustering about the name of Jean Lafitte . . . but none of them . . . equals the cold truth of his exploits at the long sandy island named Galveston."

This was the domain where the infamous pirate chieftain Jean Lafitte held sway. His base at Galveston Island was perfectly located for his many pirating forays upon the rich Spanish fleet that carried vast fortunes of gold and silver from Mexico to Spain. Their trade routes could go nowhere else than through the gauntlet provided by Lafitte and his ships manned by more than 1,000 buccaneers.

What a tremendous store of prizes Captain Lafitte must have captured! One Spanish galleon alone, the *Santa Rosa,* captured on June 12, 1816, yielded silver ingots valued at over $2,000,000.

Lafitte also had a very profitable sideline business... selling slaves. One of his best customers was Jim Bowie—that adventurous Texan who died defending the Alamo, and who is known world-wide for the knife that bears his name. It was estimated that Bowie made over $60,000 a year from selling slaves that he had bought from Lafitte.

With the money derived from selling slaves and the wealth of booty plundered from the Spanish ships, this buccaneer captain of Galveston Island must have amassed a vast fortune; some of which he hid for safe-keeping.

If the pirates did not bring treasures to the island—the hurricanes did. From Padre Island to Sabine Pass, the Texas Gulf Coast was strewn with the wrecks of many treasure-laden ships that were sunk by the fierce Gulf storms. An early map found in Bogota, Columbia, shows, in 1816, the wrecks of two vessels not more than 300 yards off the shore just south of Punta Bolivar (now Bolivar Point) where the Galveston filibusterer "Coronel Perry" was encamped, and another wreck about midway between Punta Culebra (the east end of Galveston Island) and Pelican Spit. These ships and their cargoes remain to be recovered today.

The 643-ton freighter *Laura Burnham* sank in San Luis Pass, in 1883, and on March 22, 1900, the 943-ton *Jennie Butler* went down about one mile south of the Pass. These two ships are still on the bottom of the sea.

In 1822, Stephen Austin purchased the schooner *Lively* to transport early colonists and their belongings to Texas. It was wrecked not far from San Luis Pass off the western end of Galveston Island. According to the papers of Mirabeau Buonaparte Lamar . . . "the crew was saved, but the provisions and cargo were all lost." What a cargo that must have been! In those days, the many modern methods of retrieving sunken treasure were unknown, and such cargoes were given up. The *Lively*'s rich cargo still waits to be recovered.

On December 22, 1834, Robert Kleberg, whose heirs now own one of the largest ranches in the world—the King Ranch in South Texas—and another early pioneer named VonRoeder, were shipwrecked 60 yards off shore and cast upon the beach midway down Galveston Island where . . . "3 trees were seen." This was most probably "Lafitte's Grove" which will be discussed in a later chapter. These two wealthy Texas settlers had their ship, *The Sabin*, well provided with clothes, money and equipment. This rich cargo still awaits a finder . . . just 60 yards off shore.

Dr. James Long and over 200 filibusterers lived on Bolivar Point just opposite Lafitte's fort on Galveston Island. His wife Jane became known as the "Mother of Texas" because she faithfully endured the hardships of such a life. While Lafitte was after his prey in the Gulf, Long and his henchmen seized some of the pirate's small boats that were left in the harbor at Galveston. In a letter to General E. W. Ripley at Louisiana, in 1820, Long described this action and also mentioned "the presence of some men of Mascatee who knew of $130,000 in specie buried nearby." Long was later killed in Mexico and his wife moved inland away from the rigors and hardships of island living. The $130,000 in specie (worth much more now) was never found.

Pirate booty is not the only treasure to be found around Galveston Bay. For this was the area settled by wealthy plantation owners from the South who moved all their belongings to the new land of Texas where they might set up larger dynasties.

Because of the menace from Indians, desperadoes and Mexicans, these settlers kept their money and jewels hidden or buried around their homesteads. Sometimes the owners died suddenly or were killed and the secret of their treasure location died with them. Sometimes, when danger threatened, these settlers were forced to flee in a hurry from their homes. There was no time to dig up their valuables; so they left them buried knowing that their cache would be safely hidden until their return. Some never came back.

Deaths or other series of events prevented the return of many. Others, after moving to a safer and more comfortable community, decided never again to face the terrors and hardships of early Texas living and gave up their homesteads along with their buried valuables.

A grandmother of Ivy Ilfrey who lived near Cedar Bayou in those days, said that since there were no banks at that settlement, everyone there buried his wealth for safekeeping. There are probably many of these lost treasure caches to be found.

One resident of Piney Point, west of Houston, buried $18,000 in gold during the Civil War so the Union troops would not find it. As the war progressed, his memory of the cache's location grew dimmer, and when the war was over, he was utterly confused as to the exact location. The Yankees did not get his gold—but neither did he.

In 1929, a construction crew erecting a filling station on the corner of Washington Avenue and Houston, found a pot containing $2,000 in gold buried in the ground there. Mute testimony to the treasure-burying custom of the early settlers.

Col. Ham Washington buried $4,000,000 in gold to prevent its capture by the Union Army. His fortune has not been found yet; that story will be told in a later chapter.

The biggest threat, however, to the settlers around Galveston Bay was the terrible marauding army of Mexico in 1836.

Led by General Santa Anna, this army of over 5,000 troops had already captured the town of San Antonio, destroying the Alamo fortress and killing all of its defenders, among whom were Jim Bowie, Davy Crockett and William B. Travis. Colonel Fannin and his command at Goliad were massacred and the Mexican dictator's force was on its way to capture the fleeing officials of the newly-formed Texan government, who were camped at New Washington (now Morgan's Point) on the shore of Galveston Bay. Surely, every Texas homesteader hid or buried his prized possessions in the face of such an onslaught.

One of these colonists was Enoch Brinson, who had a boat landing (Brinson Point) on San Jacinto Bay near Morgan's Point. His home was located just west of LaPorte in a grove of trees—right in line of march of the approaching Mexican Army. Being an early settler, Brinson had most certainly built up a tidy fortune. How much of it did he hide from the Mexicans? How many of Enoch Brinson's prized possessions might still be buried around that grove of trees? A treasure hunter would do well to explore that spot.

Santa Anna called himself "the Napoleon of the West", but he met his Waterloo just a few miles north of Enoch Brinson's homestead. In the afternoon of the 21st of April in 1836, General Sam Houston and his ragtag band of 783 Texans surprised a resting Mexican Army of 1,150 troops which was camped upon the plains of Saint Hyacinth (San Jacinto). After an incredibly short but fierce 18 minutes, the Mexican dictator's army was completely routed. Santa Anna was captured and made to surrender the land of Texas to a victorious army of Texans.

But something was missing. The Mexican Army was surprisingly devoid of money. Twelve thousand dollars were supposed to have been found and divided among the Texans, but several soldiers testified in court that this was not so, and that the only gold confiscated from the Mexicans was some that a dentist picked from the fillings in the teeth of dead soldiers. Did this huge army travel without any money to pay its troops? Did it not have any money with which to buy supplies along the way? Or did it loot and plunder for its needed provisions? If it *did* loot and plunder, what happened to all the prize loot of gold, silver, jewels, and other valuables taken from the hapless Texans?

The remainder of the Mexican Army (more than 2,500 troops) was encamped around Mrs. Powell's inn—about 20 leagues west of the battlefield. In charge was General Vicente Filisola, who had to beg his government for money in order to finance his retreat back to Mexico. Santa Anna *must* have taken all the money and loot with him to San Jacinto.

A personal bodyguard of Santa Anna later told that the General buried a valuable paychest full of gold, just before the battle at San Jacinto, at a spot near the battleground when he realized that a skirmish was imminent. All the other gold and loot was disposed of in quite a devious manner which will be explained in a later chapter. None of this hidden fortune was ever found.

Buried pirate booty! Sunken Spanish galleons! Rich shipwrecked cargoes! Hidden Mexican gold! Forgotten treasures! These are the many lost fortunes around Galveston Bay that are ready for the taking. The stories and legends known about these treasures and many others will be disclosed in the following chapters.

Recent progressive development in transistorized electronic equipment has produced some very sensitive metal-detecting devices. The easy availability of such equipment opens the exciting field of treasure hunting to everyone in a manner that is most fascinating. Who does not feel their blood tingle and thrill to the sound of "buried treasure"? Now it can be searched for easily with the use of these scientific instruments.

The locations disclosed in the next chapters can only be a

beginning for the serious treasure hunter. This information must be carefully analyzed, common sense applied, and a little research done before the search can actually start. Then, after a likely location is picked, the fun of treasure hunting begins for . . . .

"Treasure is where you find it!"

Chapter Two

The Legacy of Jean Lafitte

Jean Lafitte is an enigma to American history. He was at the same time a hero and a villain; a gentleman and a cad; a patriot and a subversive. None of these qualities seemed to fit him exactly, and yet, at times he exemplified each one. In his book *Doubloons* Charles B. Driscoll admits:

"If there is a more romantic figure in American history than that of Jean Lafitte, I cannot identify it."

Much could be written about this colorful piratical character, but since we are particularly interested in the treasures he left around the Galveston Bay area, we shall describe only those background events which help determine the *amounts* of treasure he could have stored up from his countless operations, and the possible *locations* of such treasures.

This enterprizing pirate leader had quite a thriving business going at his stronghold on Barataria Bay near New Orleans. In those days, New Orleans was the hub of Gulf shipping commerce and many prize-filled schooners plied the waters there. Although Lafitte did not make a practice of preying on ships that flew the flag of the United States, his plundering of English and Spanish ships did not make those countries feel too kindly toward a government that harbored such a pirate. Thus Lafitte was not on very good terms with the United States; as a matter of fact, rewards were offered by government officials for his capture.

The cold war of those days turned into a hot one with England in 1812. General Andrew Jackson, at New Orleans, met the assault of the British army standing behind crudely erected breastworks made of cotton bales. Five thousand well-trained, perfectly disciplined British troops advanced toward the General's small force; it looked like certain defeat. Suddenly, out of the marshes came help for the Americans—Jean Lafitte and his band of rascally pirates!

When the battle was over, there was no doubt in the mind of the victorious General Jackson that Jean Lafitte gave his allegiance to the United States. The United States, however, could not countenance the continued presence of this pirate mob on its shores. Lafitte would have to move on.

And so Lafitte set sail with his complete armada of ships and men. Westward went this impressive fleet, loaded to the gunwales with the booty and prizes collected from the Barataria pirate operations. It is most likely that Lafitte would not have left any of his treasures around Barataria, because the United States officials made it quite clear that he was not welcome on Yankee soil any longer. There would be no chance to come back later and recoup any hidden treasure, for Barataria was too close to New Orleans and the United States patrol boats that were based in its harbor.

There was a safer place 400 miles down the Gulf coast from which Lafitte could operate and be free from outside interference—the Spanish-held Isla Serpiente, or present-day Galveston Island. Spain was having its troubles with revolts in Mexico and Lafitte would play a masterful game of double-cross and counter-espionage between the two nations in order to give himself a free wheel at the helm of this isolated island off the Texas coast.

The buccaneer fleet rounded Punta Culebra (Snake Point) on the eastern end of Galveston Island in May of 1817. The surf of the coast side was unfit to anchor in, but around the island where the present-day harbor runs, the water was calm and deep. A perfect place for an anchorage.

About a mile and a half down the island from Snake Point there was another navigable outlet that went back out to the Gulf. Eight hundred yards from this cut, facing the calm leeward shore of the island, was an earthen fort whose walls enclosed an area of about 10,000 square feet. Those fortifications had just been abandoned by another privateer—a Frenchmen named Louis-Michel d'Aury. Aury had been pirating in the Gulf of Mexico for twelve years before he arrived at Galveston aboard his ship the *Belona*, in 1815. The Mexican revolutionists established him as the Governor of Texas, and put him in charge of 20 ships and 360 men with which he waged privateering operations against the treasure ships of Spain. One of these forays yielded $278,000 in silver and $500,000 of indigo captured from one ship alone.

After a disagreement with two other filibusterers—Francisco Mina and James Perry—Aury left Galveston and eventually set up a pirate stronghold on the island of Old Providence off the coast of Nicaragua; commanding a fleet of 14 vessels and 780 men. It is possible that he might have hidden some of his captured loot around the Galveston area. One thing is certain, he *did* leave a treasure that was found and used to a great advantage by the new pirate chieftain Jean Lafitte . . . his abandoned fortress.

This fort would become Lafitte's headquarters. It commanded a view of Galveston Bay and the harbor where he would anchor his fleet. Any approaching ships from the Gulf could easily be seen from the fort, and it also was conveniently close to two excellent avenues of escape into the Gulf—the one between Bolivar Point and the main island, and the one out the small cut which was nearby. If the enemy would come in one—Lafitte would go out the other.

Lafitte called his new town Campeche, and later changed

the name of the island to Galveston as a tribute to Count Galvez, a viceroy of Mexico, one of the countries from which he was seeking favors. Over his fort was flown the flag of Cartagena.

The large area of Galveston Bay that lay behind the island was a bonanza for pirate operations. It had many hidden upper reaches and rivers where captured ships could be taken and disposed of so that no accusing trace could be found. These same areas could also be used as hiding places for the buccaneer's ships if they were ever pursued back into the bay.

Lafitte was said to have often sailed 40 to 50 brigs, sloops and schooners up the bay and into Clear Creek, where the large trees that lined its banks would hide his tall masts from sight.

Immediately across the bay from Galveston Island was a peninsula now known as April Fool Point. Lafitte soon learned to take full advantage of its deceptive harbor whenever he was being chased. There were many hidden reefs around these waters and Lafitte knew them all. He would carefully thread his way around the point and run back and forth in the deep bay beyond. The captains of the pursuing vessels would see the upper structures and masts of his ship under full sail and thinking themselves in safe waters, run full blast across April Fool Point to catch him; unaware of the tricky shoal water these ships would suddenly run hard aground. Many an embarrassed crew would be busy trying to extricate their ship as Lafitte would cockily sail past laughing at their plight and thumbing his nose.

Inside the fort on Galveston Isle, Lafitte constructed a huge mansion for his living quarters and furnished it with all sorts of fine appointments taken from the ships that he had captured. He was extremely proud of this great house which he called his "Maison Rouge" because of its startling red color. An early 1845 map of Galveston by William H. Sandusky shows the site of this house to be between Fourteenth Street and Fifteenth Street on Avenue A.

There is an aged foundation which can be seen near this site today. This is known to be the footing left from a huge house of twelve gables built in 1878 by a retired sea captain named Hendricks. It is possible that Hendricks constructed his home directly over the original foundations of the "Maison Rouge," for in the footing walls, which are built out of a shell aggregate material similar to the type that was used in Lafitte's day, there was found some heavy iron rings which could have been used to moor ships during the pirate era.

A Houston attorney, Douglas Zwiener, became interested in Lafitte and bought the site and remains of this foundation in 1961. He hired two unemployed Negroes to clean up the site which was overgrown with weeds and littered with trash. Soon after the job was completed he happened to find out that one of the laborers had just purchased a new home that cost about $12,000 and the other helper had bought a new $14,000 house. This was quite an achievement for two men who had just recently been in the ranks of the unemployed. Was it possible that these two workers discovered some of Lafitte's buried treasure while clearing out the debris? If so, they must have done it hurriedly; one can only speculate as to what might be found with a more careful exploration of that site.

There is one report that Lafitte married Madeline Rigaud, a widow of a French settler who lived up the Trinity River, and that she died at "Maison Rouge" in 1820. Several legends tell about a huge quantity of gold being buried beneath this house with the casket of Lafitte's woman. As far as anyone knows, this was never found.

A group of Napoleon's defeated officers and several hundred Frenchmen and their families arrived at Lafitte's fort on January 15, 1818 on the schooner *Huntress*. They were seeking to establish a community settlement up the Trinity River,

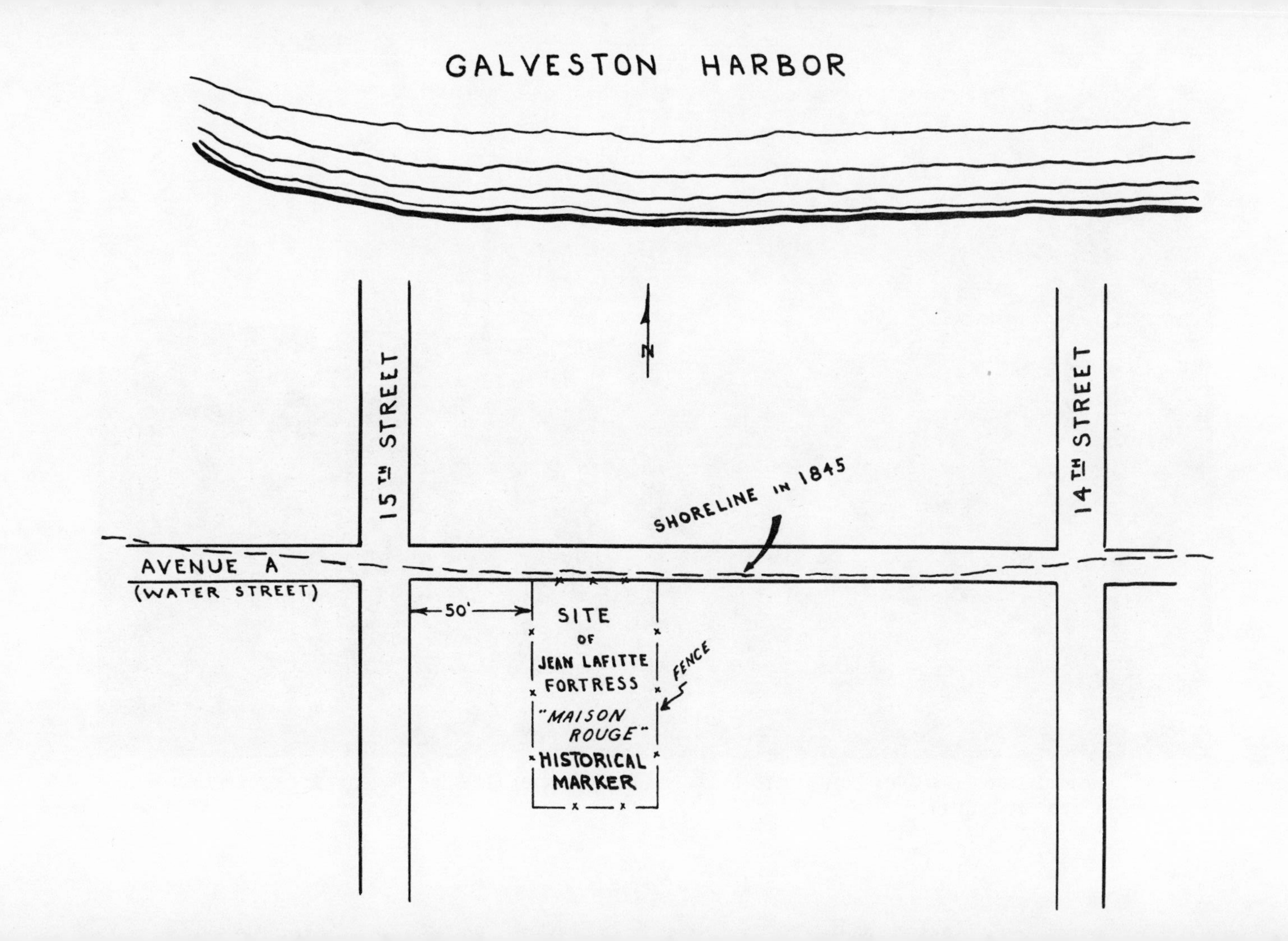
GALVESTON HARBOR
N
15TH STREET
14TH STREET
SHORELINE IN 1845
AVENUE A
(WATER STREET)
50'
SITE
OF
JEAN LAFITTE
FORTRESS
"MAISON
ROUGE"
HISTORICAL
MARKER
FENCE

Old foundations at site of Lafitte's fort—fenced in by owner Douglas Zwiener for protection from treasure hunters—1964

ostensibly to grow vineyards; however, the amount of arms and military equipment that they possessed gave away the fact that this would be the making of a French Army stronghold—designed with the purpose of rescuing Napoleon from his exile at St. Helena, invading Mexico, and establishing Joseph Bonaparte on its throne.

Lafitte sold the Frenchmen 10 large boats upon which they loaded all their money and provisions. When they set out for the journey up the bay to the Trinity, one ship was carried out to sea by a powerful outgoing tide, and it sank with all its money and supplies aboard. It was never recovered. Perhaps, one day, some lucky diver will find this ship and its historical relics.

The rest of the expedition traveled for several days up the Trinity to a large plain where they established their community which they called "Champ d' Asile" (Camp, or Field of Asylum). The hardships were too much for this group and the settlement was later abandoned. Just how much treasure was cached around this area is unknown, but it is certain that these pioneers had in their possession Napoleonic funds provided for their use, plus their own personal holdings.

One Captain Girard, who later fought in the Battle of San Jacinto, wrote that he took $500 with him to the Trinity encampment. Others with families must have carried considerably more. The area around this abandoned settlement contains many likely spots where those early inhabitants might have hidden their wealth and never came back to get it.

Lafitte would have liked for the Champ d' Asile establishment to succeed. For such a growing agricultural community would require the labor of many slaves, and slaves were his stock in trade. He could sell the slaves directly to the Frenchmen; keeping all the profits to himself by cutting out the middleman,—his friend, Jim Bowie.

A successful settlement would also bring new trade into the area . . . lots of ships loaded with money and provisions upon

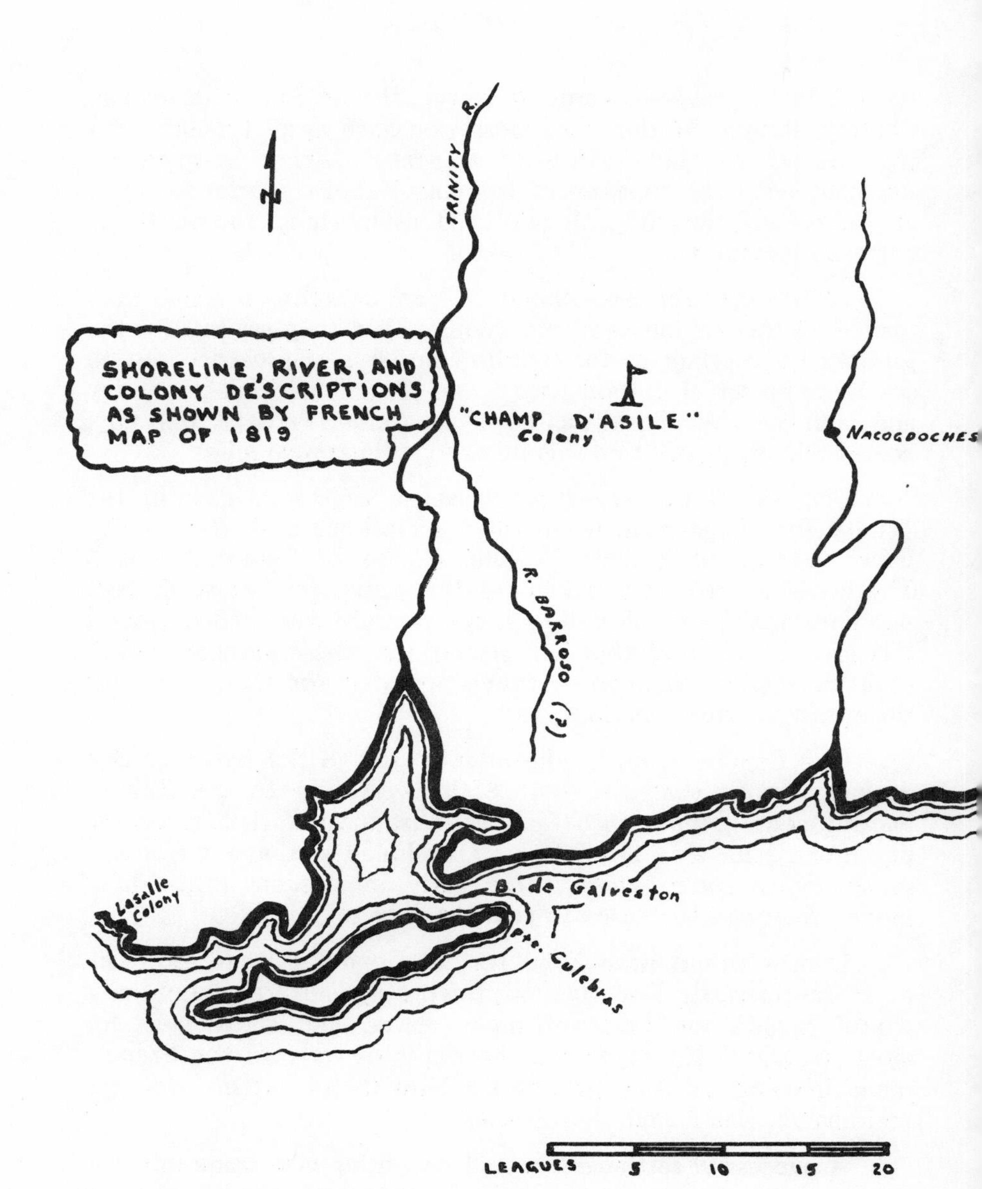

SHORELINE, RIVER, AND COLONY DESCRIPTIONS AS SHOWN BY FRENCH MAP OF 1819
TRINITY R.
"CHAMP D'ASILE" Colony
NACOGDOCHES
R. BARROSO (?)
B. de Galveston
Lasalle Colony
Pta. Culebras
LEAGUES 5 10 15 20

Site of Napoleonic Champ d' Asile is somewhere on the left bank below this spot on the Trinity River at Liberty, Texas.

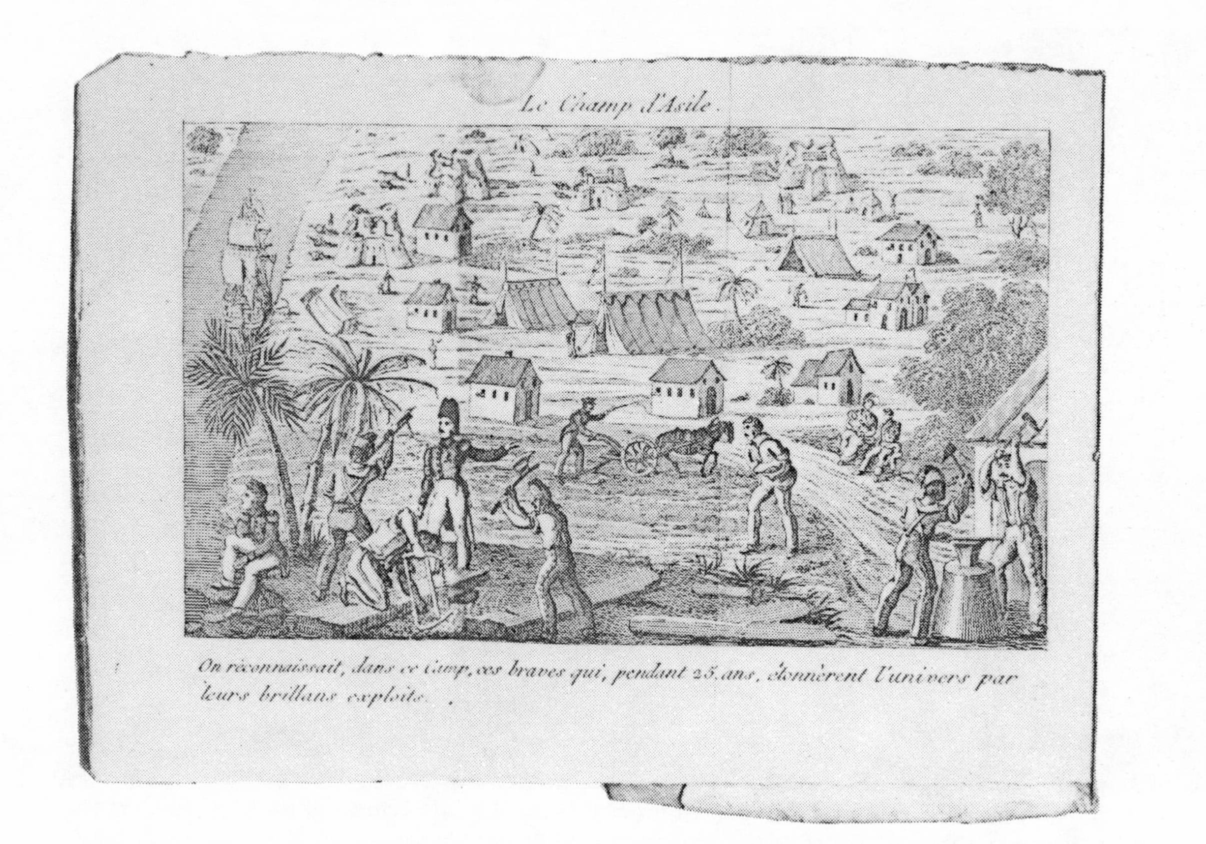

Life at Champ d' Asile as depicted on frontispiece of book published in Paris in 1820.

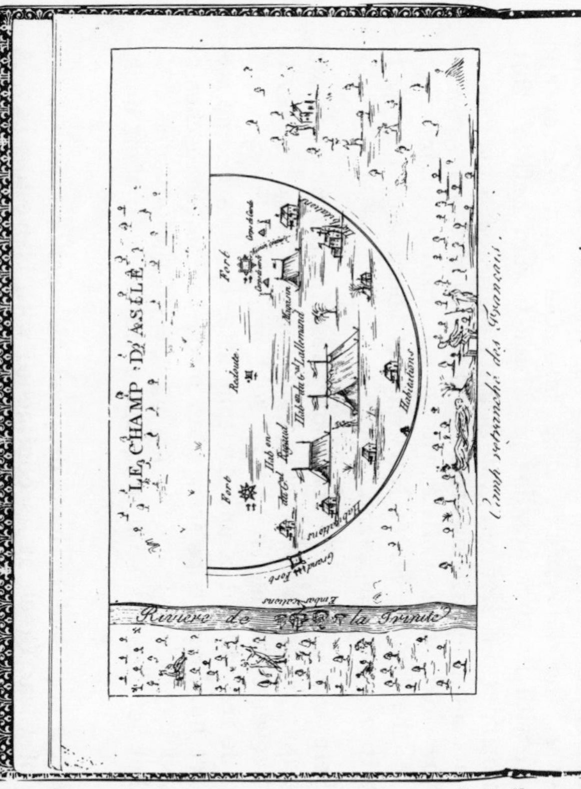

L'HÉROÏNE

DU TEXAS,

OU

VOYAGE DE MADAME ***

AUX ÉTATS-UNIS ET AU MEXIQUE.

Orné d'une Gravure représentant le Champ d'Asile et le Camp retranché des Français.

Cet Ouvrage est terminé par une Romance.

PAR Mr G...n. F......n.

A PARIS,

CHEZ PLANCHER, ÉDITEUR DU MANUEL DES BRAVES, rue Poupée, n° 7.

1819.

Fortifications and layout of Champ d' Asile as shown on frontispiece of French publication in 1819.

which he could prey and further fill his larder. But since the Trinity encampment failed, he had to be content with the plunder of the rich Spanish fleet that was busy transporting gold and silver to Spain from the Gulf ports of Central America and Mexico.

Lafitte spent most of his time governing Galveston Island, while his sub-captains searched the waters of the Gulf for such prizes. Some of his captains grew too greedy, however, and attacked several ships flying the flag of the United States. This angered Lafitte so much, that he hung several of these freebooters on the duelling field of Pelican Island, just across the harbor from his fort.

Shortly thereafter, in January of 1821, a United States brig-of-war, the *Enterprize* sailed into Galveston harbor and anchored with its guns bristling broadside toward Lafitte's fort. Its commander, Lt. Kearney, told Lafitte that he and his gang of cutthroats must leave Galveston Island within sixty days or they would be fired upon. Lafitte was in no position to incur the wrath of the United States Navy—he set about immediately to prepare to evacuate the island.

There would only be room on the ships for his men and the necessary supplies to provide them for their long journey to their next destination. The heavy gold and silver booty would have to be transported at another time after their new camp was firmly set up. Many trips were then made to the far reaches of Galveston Bay, away from the prying eyes of the outsiders . . . ships that left loaded with loot, and returned with their decks empty.

Lafitte was said to have dropped his anchor often at the mouth of Clear Creek at its confluence with Galveston Bay. A chest laden with gold and silver would be loaded on a small boat, and Lafitte with a small crew would disappear up the creek out of sight of the larger ship. Later they would return after having buried the booty.

Did Lafitte row back alone? Did he dispose of his treasure-packing crew in the usual buccaneer custom . . . "dead men tell no tales?"

He most probably did not, for he was not known to be a bloodthirsty man, and the practice of killing his crew would certainly make it hard to enlist help for any subsequent burying trips. Therefore, *some* of Lafitte's crew surely knew of his treasure locations. A number of his henchmen decided to give up the life of pirating and planned to move inland to a more honest means of making a living. Lafitte must have made sure that all of those who knew of his treasure locations would sail with him and not be left behind where they could dig up the booty for themselves. He later told a native of Florida that he had left enough gold buried in Texas to build a solid gold bridge across the Mississippi River.

According to an eye-witness, on March 3, 1821, Jean Lafitte, dressed simply in a foraging cap and a blue frock coat "of a most villainous fit" boarded a brig of 200 tons and 16 cannons and set sail again for the open gulf. The town of Campeche was a burning torch in the background, for as he left, Lafitte set fire to everything including his beloved "Maison Rouge."

The swashbuckling pirate sailed away out of history, never to be heard from again.

Myriad legends abound concerning his death: Perished in a hurricane off the Yucatan Peninsula; killed in a battle on a sandbank called Blanquilla near the Mexican Island of Contoy; captured and killed during an engagement with a United States revenue cutter in Lavaca Bay, Texas; in 1826, died of fever and buried at the Mexican coast town of Dzilan de Bravo; died and buried under a hecatomb of turtle shells at the village of Dolores on Isla Mujeres, near Cancun, Mexico; yet a Lafitte family Bible, letters, documents, and a handwritten 257-page journal of memoirs all signed by "Jn Laffite"—acquired in the summer of

1976 by Texas State Supreme Court Justice Price Daniel, former. Governor of Texas—present evidence of the pirate Jean Lafitte eventually assuming the name of John Lafflin, settling in the United States and dying at Alton, Illinois in 1854.

One of the most intriguing stories of Lafitte's death was related in 1928, by Dr. Louis Genella, of New Orleans. In the attic of a very distinguished family of that city, he found some faded documents in an old chest that revealed a geneology of Jean Lafitte, and his subsequent fate.

Dr. Genella's research established that Lafitte was a cousin of Napoleon Bonaparte and a nephew of John Paul Jones, and that, in 1819, the corsair rescued Napoleon from his exile in St. Helena—leaving an imposter in his place. The former emperor died at sea, and Lafitte buried him in Louisiana, where Goose Bayou intersected the Bayou Barataria. Lafitte also voyaged to the little Breton village where his uncle John Paul Jones was buried, and brought his body back to rebury it beside Napoleon's Louisiana grave.

Later, after Lafitte was killed during a fight with a British ship, in the Gulf of Mexico, *his* body was buried beside his cousin's and uncle's; so according to Dr. Genella, on a high bank in the marshes of Louisiana, an old iron cross marks the final resting place of Emperor Napoleon Bonaparte, Admiral John Paul Jones and pirate Jean Lafitte.

Whatever his demise, this American buccaneer certainly left his mark on the island of Galveston, but more than that, he left a legend of untold treasures buried around the shores of Galveston Bay—awaiting his return.

Chapter Three

Island Secrets

The night before Jean Lafitte parted from Galveston Island, he was seen walking to and fro upon the floors of his "Maison Rouge" murmuring something about . . . "My treasure . . . the three trees." He must surely have been distraught at the thought of leaving his island fortress and possibly a little out of his head; so those that heard him thought that he had unknowingly revealed the location of one of his treasures.

The three trees . . . Lafitte's Grove.

Midway down the island, three windswept trees marked the site of an earlier bloody battle between Lafitte's pirates and a tribe of Karankawa Indians. After three days of fighting, seven pirates and sixty Indians were killed. The defeated Indians left the island and never came back. This battlefield was soon known as "Lafitte's Grove."

Upon hearing about ". . . treasure . . . the three trees . . ." those henchmen Lafitte left behind wasted no time and rushed to Lafitte's Grove to recover some of their hard-earned booty. They searched and dug diligently, only finding a few scattered gold doubloons until suddenly, one of their shovels struck a solid object buried deep in the sand. The shoveling became more frantic as a large brass-banded wooden box gradually appeared out of the excavation. This was it! Booty for all! Lafitte's treasure!

The excited pirates quickly broke open the cover of the chest in anticipation of the riches therein, but were amazed at

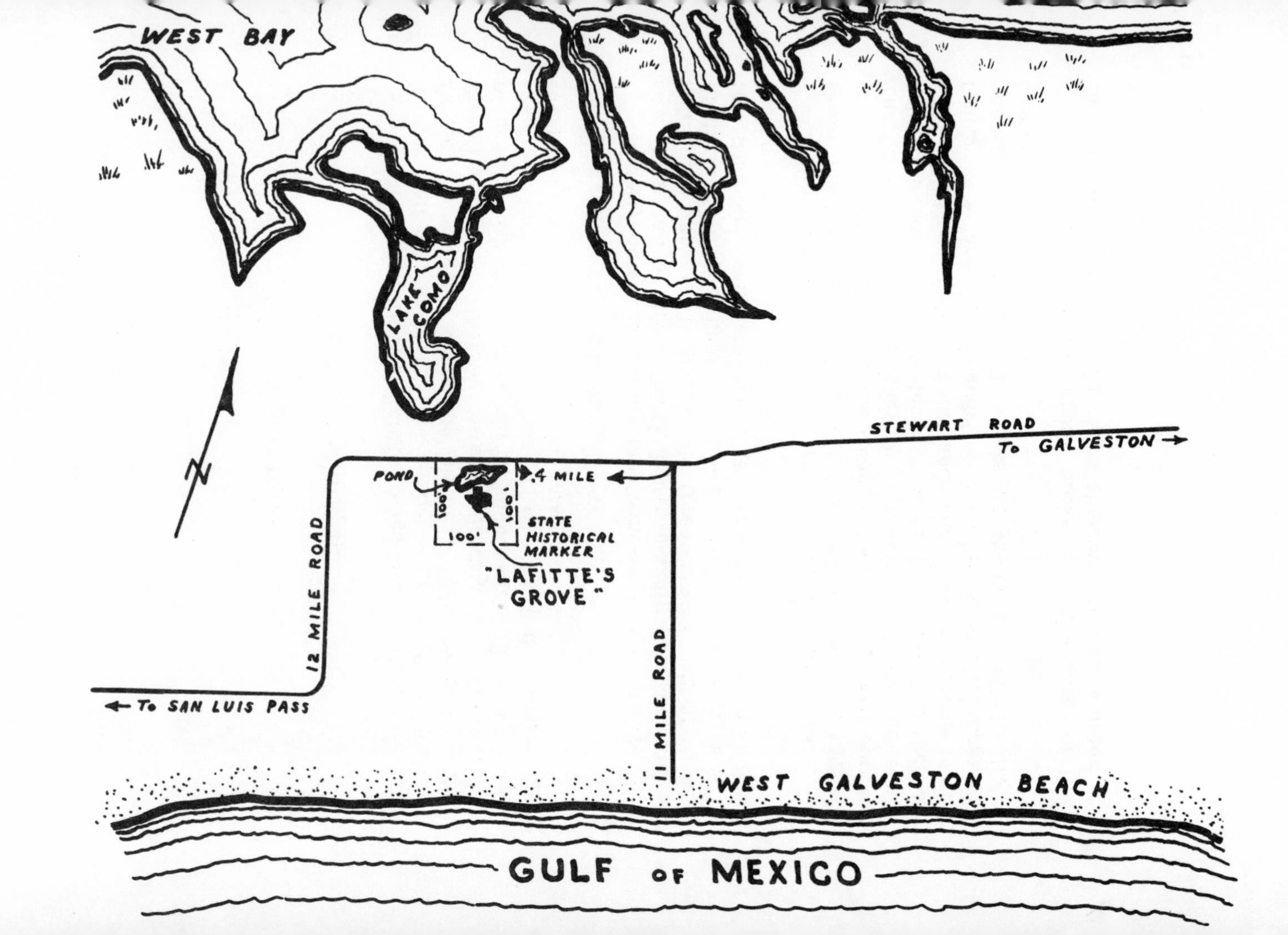
WEST BAY
LAKE COMO
STEWART ROAD
To GALVESTON
POND
.4 MILE
100'
100'
100'
STATE HISTORICAL MARKER
"LAFITTE'S GROVE"
12 MILE ROAD
To SAN LUIS PASS
11 MILE ROAD
WEST GALVESTON BEACH
GULF OF MEXICO

Lafitte's Grove

what they saw . . . only the remains of the corpse of a woman were lying in the chest! No gold. No silver. Shocked and disappointed, they continued digging around the grove, but nothing else was found.

Did not Lafitte have a wife whom he could have considered his "treasure?" Was this what he was referring to on that restless night back at the "Maison Rouge?" Or was it possible that there might be another *treasure* at some other *trees*? Strange markings were found on some trees near Seabrook, where Lafitte was known to have anchored his ships, and there are some people who believe that Lafitte hid a treasure near three large trees on the high banks of Lone Oak Bayou. The majority of opinion, however, seems to favor Lafitte's Grove as a hiding place. Galveston historian J. O. Dyer, for instance, related that the pirate chieftain buried an Indian and three oaken casks full of gold at the grove, and two ex-Lafitte pirates named Roach and Franks, who lived at Anahuac in 1830, reported that their leader had hidden his ill-gotten gains near the three trees that formed the grove on the western end of Galveston Island.

There is another story of Lafitte's returning to Galveston Island, shortly after he left, to bury a chest full of gold and jewels at the grove. For a marker, he buried a brass surveying rod known as a "Jacob's Staff" and left about a foot of it sticking out of the sand. It is possible that the blowing sands soon covered the rod and those who were to look later for treasure at the grove never ran across the marker.

The three trees at Lafitte's Grove were destroyed by a hurricane in 1915. After a number of years, young new sprouts finally grew out of the old gnarled roots, and today quite a few small trees remain at the spot. The grove is located about fifty yards east of Stewart's Road about twelve miles down the island adjoining the W. Ostermeyer property. A State of Texas historical marker can be found among the weeds and bushes that grow around the grove.

Within a short walking distance from Lafitte's Grove, a farmer named Bill Zingleman was plowing in a rented cabbage patch one September day in 1937. He saw something shining in the dirt, and with a closer look, discovered it to be a silver dollar. Scratching around further in the soil, Zingleman found many more loosely buried coins; finally he unearthed a whole glass jar full of silver coins. In it were old French and Spanish coins, and several American quarters, half dollars and dollars. The coins, dated from 1822 to 1897, place the burial date of this cache at a time in history when there was no threat of Indians, Mexicans, Union troops or the like. Just another buried treasure that someone had forgotten about.

There is also the story of an old recluse woman who lived out on the island who buried a jar full of jewels near her house. She died suddenly from a severe illness while she was alone at her place out on the island. The secret of the hiding place of her jewels died with her. They were never found.

Early in 1836, some Galveston Island inhabitants were looking for some building materials around some wreckage piles of ship timbers that had drifted up on the sand dunes of West Beach. They had to dig out some of the heavier timbers and about three feet below the surface they came upon a large quantity of silver plate. Greatly excited, they dug up the whole area and their further explorations uncovered three gold Spanish doubloons.

A monstrous September hurricane in 1818 forced Lafitte's fleet of ships to seek the shelter of his harbor. From all parts of the Gulf they ran before the wind in a race for the protection of Galveston Island. The hurricane hit with a fury that would not allow any of the ships to unload the prizes that had been captured out in the Gulf. The pirates were more concerned with their lives, and hurriedly took refuge in the fort. Most of the vessels were overturned and sunk in the harbor; several broke loose from their moorings and were driven aground on Virginia Point and destroyed there with their gold and silver booty.

The bottom of Galveston Bay still holds the wealth of cargo that went down with these ships and the many other prize-laden vessels that met ill fate upon the treasure island of Galveston.

In the mid-1800's, at the huge Jackson ranch on Double Bayou, there appeared two seafaring men who asked permission to camp along the bayshore for a few days of fishing. Permission being granted, these piratical-looking characters drove their wagon off and camped along the bayshore in the lower end of the pasture.

Several days later, they left the ranch in a hurry—driving their wagon away at full speed as if they were being chased. They did not even stop at the ranchhouse as they went by. Their departure looked so suspicious, that an investigation was made of their campgrounds. Several freshly dug holes were discovered in the vicinity of the shoreline and in the largest hole was left an impression of a large square chest that had evidently been taken out. The two sea-faring men were never seen again—they had evidently found what they were looking for and left! If it *was* a treasure chest, would it not be possible that this same area might contain other treasures? Only the vanished buccaneer Jean Lafitte would have had the answer. His failure to return leaves a mystery as to how much pirate gold *still* lies buried around Galveston Bay.

A rich Spanish prize ship full of treasure was said to be scuttled by Lafitte in Galveston Bay during a battle with the Spaniards. That certain vessel and its cargo has never been recovered.

This information was made known in the mid-1800's by a Galveston resident who claimed to be Lafitte's cabin boy in earlier times. That same gentleman also revealed a most curious story regarding the life and death of the pirate chieftain, as follows:

Mortimer Wilson was an upcoming young businessman in

Charleston, South Carolina, when he became engaged to marry a beautiful girl of the local society. One of the lady's previous suitors, however, in a jealous rage, attacked Wilson with the result that the attacker was accidently killed with his own pistol. Fleeing from the scene, Wilson eventually ended up as a privateer, serving under Jean Lafitte.

The pirate captain quickly realized the potential leader material in the well-educated young man and proceeded to adopt him as his "nephew", make him his protegé, and train him to be his second-in-command.

One day, near Vera Cruz, a rich Spanish ship was sighted and Lafitte turned the command of his vessel over to Wilson to take the prize. The young Lieutenant audaciously attacked and captured the ship in the midst of an escorting squadron of man-of-wars. Boarding her with a prize crew the pirates hurriedly began sailing away from the formidably armed Spanish fleet.

A fierce running battle was fought all the way across the Gulf of Mexico to the harbor at Galveston where the privateers and their prize ship—closely pursued by the Spaniards—entered into the bay. There, in order to elude their enemy, the pirates scuttled their prize ship and then sailed up into the shallow waters of the bay where the deep-drafted men-of-war could not follow. The Spanish crafts turned about and departed to seek more sea room, leaving the buccaneers safe from their vengeful guns.

During the sea-fight, Lafitte was killed by a stray shot and, after the battle was over, the officers and men who had cruised under him elected Mortimer Wilson to be their new chief. Since he had been acknowledged to be Lafitte's nephew and as the pirate captain always called him "Lafitte", the crew knew Wilson by no other name; so he continued the deception and thereafter commanded the privateers calling himself "Jean Lafitte".

After the Battle of New Orleans, Wilson *alias* Lafitte

married a lady of Charleston, South Carolina and settled in Savannah, Georgia. He soon became restless and again turned to piracy as the commander of the privateers at Galveston Island. After abandoning Galveston in 1821, he also abandoned his name of Lafitte and once again became a peaceful citizen named Mortimer Wilson. The mortal remains of Jean Lafitte, or Mortimer Wilson, now rest in a quiet grave near Savannah.

Lafitte's ex-cabin boy claimed that he knew the exact location of the sunken prize ship and its treasures that Wilson/Lafitte sent to the bottom of Galveston Bay. He also stated that Lafitte's men had a favorite burying place for their loot up Hitchcock's (Highlands) Bayou at the high ground near Schmidt's Garden and that a portion of those treasures had already been found.

Is the Mortimer Wilson revelation a fact, or is it just another one of the many legends that have grown about the colorful Jean Lafitte? Charles W. Hayes, author of the fine two-volume *History of the Island and the City of Galveston* (1879), seemed to believe it true.

Another such story, or legend, concerns the beautiful but poisonous oleander bush that grows on Galveston Island. So prolific and charming are these red and white flowering shrubs, that Galveston is often called "the Oleander City". It is said that Jean Lafitte is responsible for bringing the oleander to the island and giving it a name.

During a sea raid on a Norwegian schooner, he captured one passenger who kept clinging to an unusual flowering plant. This victim, whose name was Ole Anderson, became Lafitte's gardener and the pirates all called him "Ole Ander". His pretty bush flourished in the mild, moist Gulf climate and Galveston Island gradually became a flower pot of beauty as Ole's plantings took over. Lafitte thought it only appropriate to honor his gardener by naming the plant for him—the oleander.

There is a romantic legend that under each red oleander

bush, a pirate treasure is buried. This may not be too far wrong, for one of Lafitte's favorite lieutenants named Lambert, testified that the buccaneers had buried much of their ill-gotten booty on the oleander-dotted island of Galveston.

Chapter Four

Pirate Plunder

Lafitte, when ordered to leave Galveston, was supposed to have loaded his flagship, the *Pride,* with five bearskins full of gold, and sailed somewhere into the back reaches of Galveston Bay to bury the gold. His ship ran aground and developed such a leak that it sank up in the mouth of a small lake. The heavily loaded ship settled down into the muddy bottom before the gold could be taken off. This treasure was never found or recovered.

In the summer of 1949, B. J. Krigar and Leo T. Behne advertised in a Houston newspaper that they had a metal detecting instrument and offered to share the proceeds with anyone who would furnish them with a good buried treasure location. E. H. Sherman of Wallisville remembered that his grandfather had discovered a sunken ship in Lake Miller in 1883. It was hidden just below the surface of the water, and snagged on to some logs that he was floating down to the Trinity River. Sherman's sister, Mrs. E. H. Clark, recalled her father taking her to the sunken ship several times and that one day he marked its location by driving a large iron spike into an oak tree. Sherman and his sister got in touch with the two treasure hunters and after a two-months' search they finally located the ship—less than 200 feet from the bank of a 20-foot wide channel that connected Lake Charlotte with the Trinity River.

The hulk of this ship had sunk over eight feet down into the quicksand-like mud of Lake Miller. By using a 10½-foot-

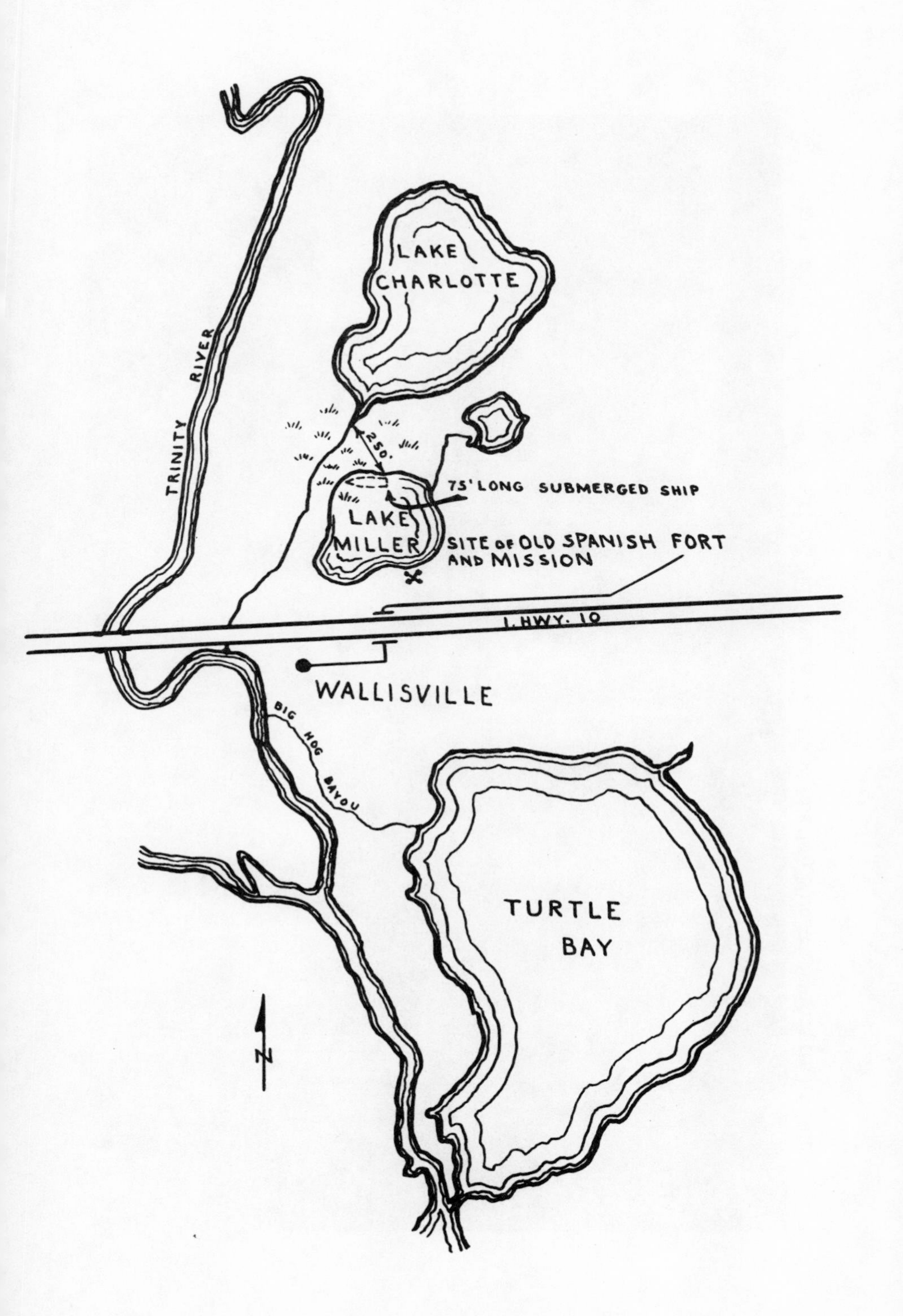
LAKE CHARLOTTE
TRINITY RIVER
250'
75' LONG SUBMERGED SHIP
LAKE MILLER
SITE OF OLD SPANISH FORT AND MISSION
I. HWY. 10
WALLISVILLE
BIG HOG BAYOU
TURTLE BAY
N

Near bank of Lake Miller is site of old Spanish fort and Mission Nuestra Senora de La Luz.

long pipe as a probe, they were able to stake out an outline of the ship. It measured roughly 75 feet long by about 35 feet wide. A measurement that could have fit the *Pride*!

A man named John Lafitte of St. Joseph, Missouri, who said he was a descendant of Lafitte, heard about this discovery and came to Houston to claim his rights to anything that was found. He had information that, besides gold, the *Pride* also had aboard a 42,000-word manuscript written by Lafitte about his exploits. He seemed more interested in the manuscript than in the five bearskins full of gold. But as the treasure-hunting party turned a deaf ear to this claimant, the State of Texas turned the lock on any further digging in the lake. It seems that the proper leasing procedure of state-owned lands had not been complied with, and the expedition was ordered to stop its exploration. As far as anyone knows, the treasures of gold and history that may lie beneath the sunken ship timbers in Lake Miller have never been recovered.

Across Trinity Bay on the west side of the shore at the Morgan's Point ferryboat landing, a state highway crew came upon some old ship's timbers in March of 1950 while dredging in the water for a ferry parking area. A solid pine keel, about 65 feet long, and some ribs were pulled out of the mire. The fact that these timbers contained no nails, but were put together with square handmade spikes, placed the ship's vintage back to the time of Lafitte. Again, the size of this vessel make it possible that this might have been the wreckage of the *Pride*. If so, the five bearskins full of gold and Lafitte's manuscript may still be waiting in the mud at Morgan's Point for further explorations to uncover them.

A Spanish schooner was trapped and sunk by the Gulf pirates up Old River, north of Trinity Bay, that had aboard a cannon filled with gold. Lacking modern-day diving equipment, the pirates were never able to retrieve the heavy gold-filled gun. There are stories of other treasures that were plundered by the pirates being buried along the cliff-like banks of the river. The many caves and holes along those banks, testify that someone is still trying to find that loot.

There is a legend of several large strongboxes, filled with gold, being buried near Barber's Hill. These have never been found; yet the pock-marked fields around this area give evidence that treasure hunters will not easily give up their search for that fortune.

The vicinities of Goose Creek and Cedar Bayou were known to be some of Lafitte's favorite haunts, and the mouth of the San Jacinto River was used as a careening place for repairing and watering his ships.

There were no shipyards available in those days; so in order to repair the bottom of a ship's hull, it had to be taken to quiet waters where it could be beached close to shore. The crew would then fasten lines to the tops of the masts, and stretch them to a gang of men on shore, who would heave slowly on them. The leverage thus applied would "careen" or lay the ship over on its side. The bottom would then be accessible above the water and ready to be repaired or cleaned.

Close to the San Jacinto River careening place was an old river channel, where speedboat races are now held. In the southeastern part of this body of water, the pirates supposedly sank a brass cannon filled with gold. Nearby, on the north shore of Lost Lake, ruins of fortress walls and cannon emplacements can still be found—mute evidence of the pirate domain.

In 1875, an Englishman named John Wight, and several other men came to this area with an old map showing the location of a buried treasure. Everything on the map checked out with the geography thereabouts, except that the main marker was missing. It was a cedar tree with two crossed pegs driven into it. There was no such cedar tree to be found.

Uncle Bill Miller, who was a long-time resident of Old River, remembered that when he was a boy, he had cut down a cedar tree that had *two crossed pegs* in it, one day when he was coon hunting. He offered to show Wight the location of the tree if Wight would show him the map and split the treasure fifty-fifty. The Englishman refused—hoping eventually to come upon the remains of the tree, and thus keeping all the treasure to himself. He kept searching for many years and finally died without finding anything.

There is another legend of two cannons being filled with gold and heaved into the Buffalo Bayou near Lynchburg, and the deep waters at the mouth of Cedar Bayou are *said* to rush over the final resting place of several other gold-filled cannons.

Chapter Five

Gold Is Where the Pirates Were

When the bucaneer village of Campeche, on Galveston Island was disbanded, there were some freebooters who did not go to sea with Lafitte. Most of them came inland and settled around the area where the towns of Kemah and Seabrook are now located. Their descendants still live in these small villages and the cemeteries there have many tombstones that are engraven with the names of the remnants of Lafitte's pirate gang. Even the street names such as "Kipp" in Kemah, reflect the influence that these ex-Lafitte henchmen had on the area.

One of these pirates, named Jim Campbell, settled 15 miles south of Seabrook on a bayou that was later to bear his name—Campbell's Bayou.

Another one of Lafitte's lieutenants named Taylor, built his home on a small lake that emptied into Clear Lake. His wife was buried on the north shores of what was later called Taylor Lake. Lafitte would often drop his anchor near the outlet to that lake, and Taylor had evidently marked it in his mind for future use.

How strange it was, that the remainder of Lafitte's pirates seemed to cluster in this particular area. What could have been the secret, held by the shores of Clear Creek, that attracted them? Were the pirates hoping to find Lafitte's buried treasure close by?

Jesse A. Ziegler recalled that when he was a boy he remembered seeing many of the men of Lafitte's gang. There was one old pirate called "Crazy Ben" who stuck most vividly in his memory. Ben was a fisherman who lived on the bay near what is now the town of Seabrook, in about 1856. He was a typical Lafitte buccaneer, complete with earrings, mustache and long sideburns.

One day when he was fishing in the bay, a porpoise began playing around his skiff. Hoping to get rid of this pest that was scaring his fish away, Ben threw a harpoon at him. He was a better shot than he thought, for the lance pierced the porpoise's hide and stuck there. This would not have mattered much, except that the harpoon was fastened by a chain to the bow of the boat, and the porpoise decided to get away from there—and get away fast! So avast and away went the demon, over 30 miles per hour, dragging behind him a bewildered man and his skiff. Some men in another boat finally rescued Ben up in the far eastern reaches of Galveston Bay.

Old Ben would often come to Houston to buy supplies, visit the bars around Commerce and Congress Avenues, and get drunk. He would always buy his drinks and supplies with old Spanish and Mexican coins. He seemed to have an unlimited supply of this money. Everyone suspected that Ben had found one of Lafitte's hidden treasures, since fishing in those days was not very profitable, and certainly no one would be *giving* Ben valuable old Spanish coins.

Several times, when Ben seemed to be especially "in his cups," men would follow him home, hoping that he might lead them to the treasure. But Ben was not as crazy as his name led them to believe. He would always lead his trackers around different routes, losing them, and keeping the location of his treasure a mystery. His followers, however, did find some strange markings on several trees along Clear Creek, just out of Seabrook, but that was all.

Ben's secret died with him one day, when his drowned body was found on the shore at the mouth of Clear Creek. Foul play was suspected, but no one cared much about Ben—only in his treasure!

Mrs. Rockwell Hoskins, a native of Goose Creek, told of a noted recluse that lived near the mouth of Goose Creek, who was believed to have been one of Lafitte's buccaneers. He hunted game in the winter, fished in the summer, farmed the seasons in between, and pretty well lived a life of ease. He must have been aware of where some of Lafitte's treasure was hidden, for he would disappear for a week or more (enough time to travel to Clear Creek and back?) and then reappear with his pockets filled with gold and silver Spanish coins. No one was ever able to find out where his secret cache of treasure was hidden.

In the early sixties a villainous-looking, dark complexioned foreigner often appeared in Houston to buy supplies. He always paid for them out of a bag containing a quantity of ancient dated gold and silver Spanish coins. He was one-eyed and had a scar from a saber or knife slashed across his cheek. He was thought to be one of Lafitte's pirates who lived in the vicinity of Clear Creek, but he kept to himself, and no one could find out much about him.

In January of 1965, a youth who was searching with a metal detector along the banks of Clear Creek in Seabrook found some gold and silver Spanish coins dated from 1790 to 1806. These coins were buried about 11 inches beneath the surface of the ground. Further digging at this spot uncovered the lower part of a human jawbone—with several teeth still attached to it. Grass roots had completely entwined the bone and its cavities.

Oddly enough, in about 1930, a commercial fisherman, Wesley Müecke pulled up a human skull in his nets while seining in Clear Creek exactly in front of the spot where the jawbone

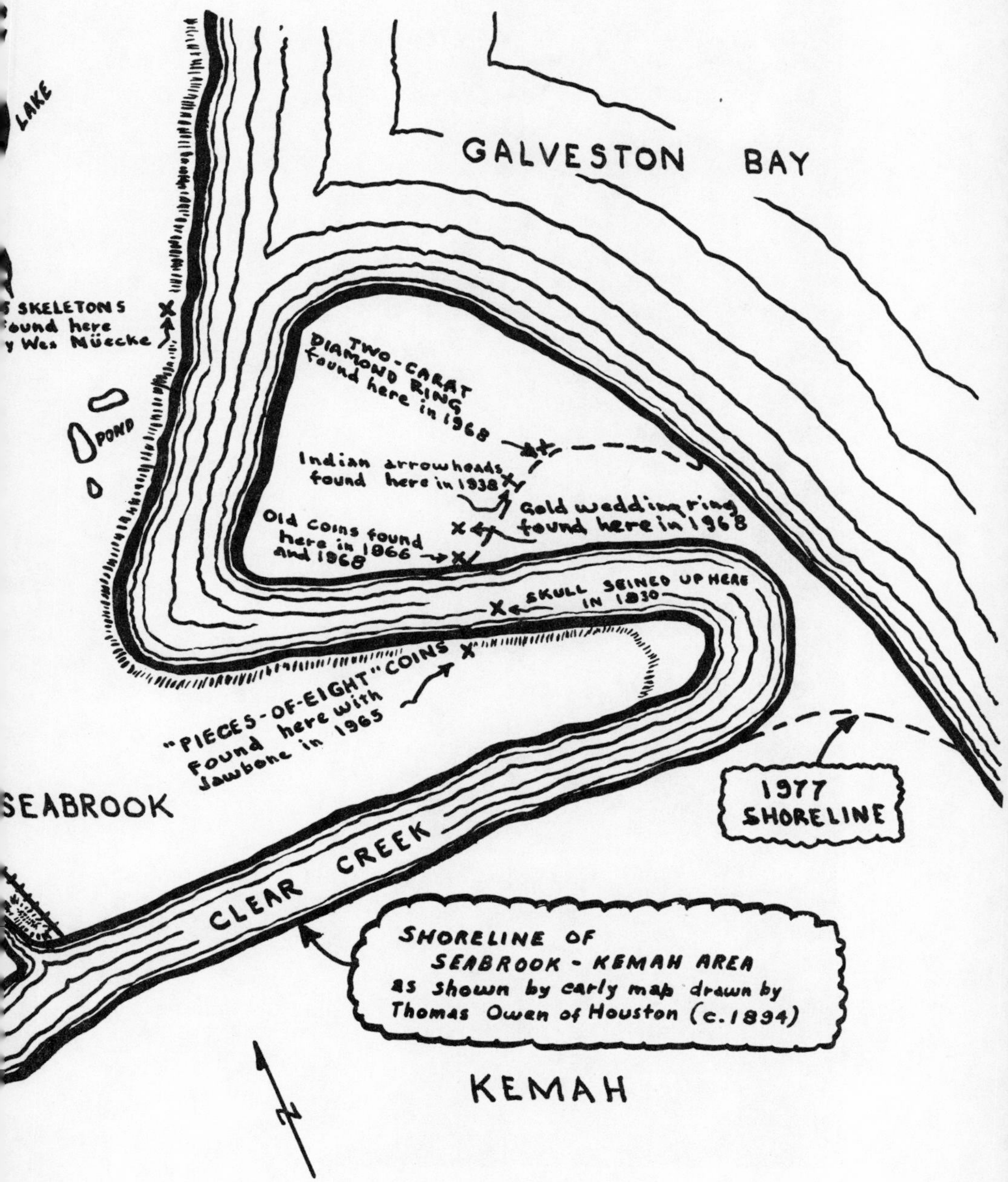

GALVESTON BAY

LAKE

SKELETONS
found here
Wes Müecke

POND

TWO-CARAT
DIAMOND RING
found here in 1968

Indian arrowheads
found here in 1938

Gold wedding ring
found here in 1968

Old coins found
here in 1966
and 1968

SKULL SEINED UP HERE
IN 1830

"PIECES-OF-EIGHT" COINS
found here with
Jawbone in 1965

SEABROOK

1977
SHORELINE

CLEAR CREEK

SHORELINE OF
SEABROOK - KEMAH AREA
as shown by early map drawn by
Thomas Owen of Houston (c.1894)

N

KEMAH

Island at mouth of Clear Creek between Seabrook and Kemah.

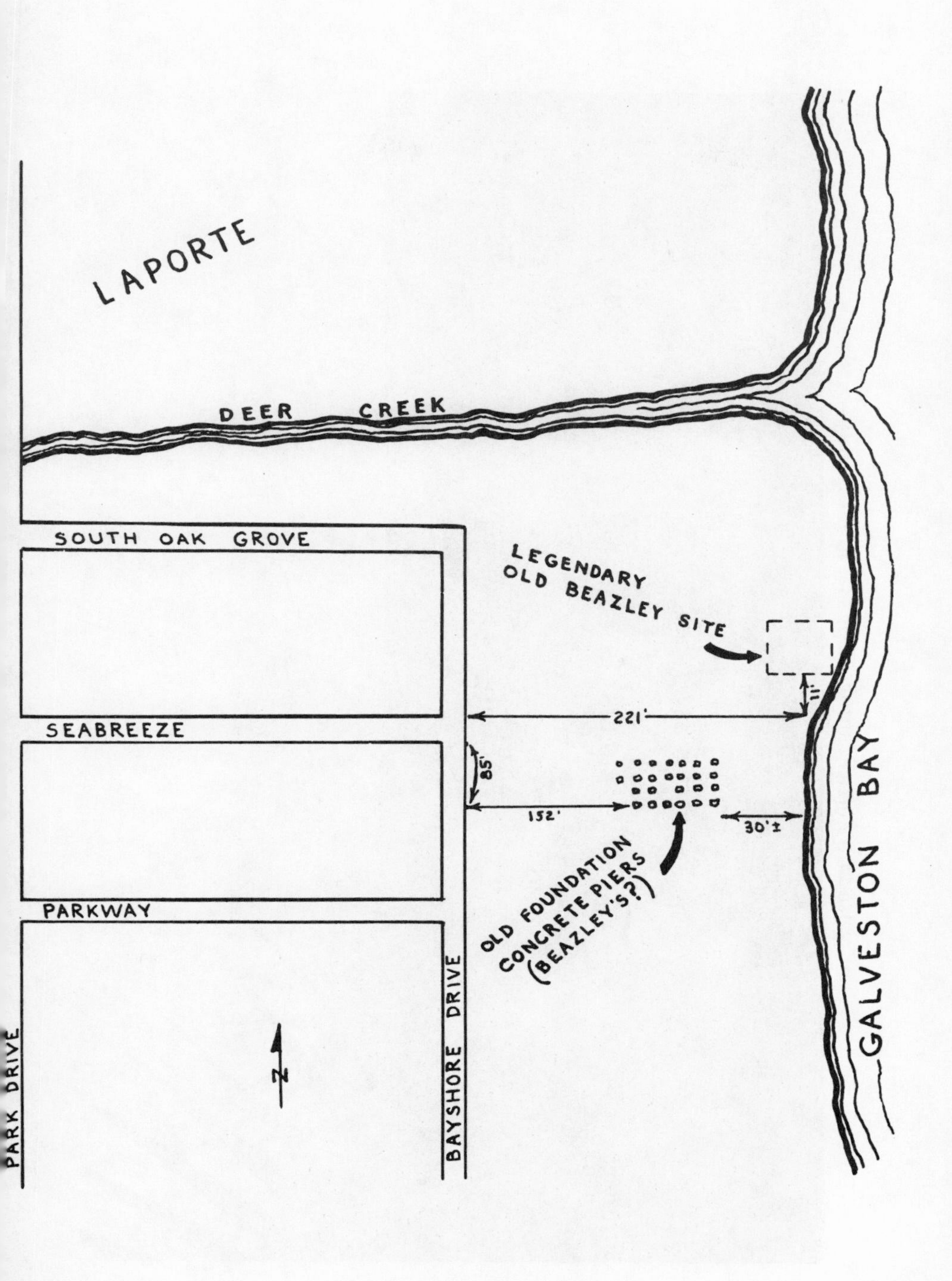
LAPORTE
DEER CREEK
SOUTH OAK GROVE
SEABREEZE
PARKWAY
PARK DRIVE
BAYSHORE DRIVE
LEGENDARY
OLD BEAZLEY SITE
11'
221'
85'
152'
30'±
OLD FOUNDATION
CONCRETE PIERS
(BEAZLEY'S?)
GALVESTON BAY
N

Waterfront at legendary John Beazley homesite.

and coins were found. Directly across the creek from this spot, Buck Rankin and his wife found a handful of old coins while searching for driftwood in the summer of 1966.

This location was not too far from the mouth of Clear Creek—just a convenient rowing distance where Lafitte might have put his small boat ashore and hurriedly buried his chest of gold. Could these loose coins have spilled out? Does the rest of Lafitte's treasure lie buried somewhere nearby?

J. Frank Dobie, in his book *Coronado's Children,* tells of a weary traveler on horseback, fording the mouth of a small stream at Galveston Bay, south of La Porte, shortly after the Civil War. Finding a large house on the other side, he tied his horse out in the barn and lay down to rest in one of the empty rooms. Later on in the night, he was awakened by a noise, and standing over him was a ghostly apparition wearing the garb of a pirate, pointing to the ground and saying, "Under this house is buried more gold than is good for any man!" The apparition went on to say that he was the ghost of Lafitte, and was doomed to remain at that house until he could find a worthy man who would take his treasure and put it to good use. The frightened traveler stayed long enough to get over his shock and then high-tailed it away from that haunted house as fast as he could.

In recounting his story later, it was supposed that he had stopped at the old Beazley house which was located on the bayshore next to Little Deer Creek near La Porte. It was right along this shore line that a boy found an old Spanish coin at the water's edge in 1948.

Shortly before 1950, a man from Humble was digging for this legendary treasure around the old Beazley house. It was during the month of June, and he dug in the cool night by the light of the moon, to escape the sultry summer heat. After digging a waist-deep hole, he grew tired and lay down to nap. He was soon awakened by hearing a thin wailing voice calling his name, and as he opened his eyes, there appeared before him a beautiful young woman dressed in strange flowing garments. He asked who she was and she replied "Theodosia Burr—I have come to show you where the treasure is."

The man was so exhausted from his previous labors that he told her to wait until after he had rested. But as he closed his eyes again, he suddenly recalled that Theodosia Burr was the daughter of Aaron Burr. In 1812 she had sailed from Charleston, was lost at sea, and never heard from again. Could her ship have met up with the pirate Jean Lafitte? Could she have been the beautiful girl whom Lafitte supposedly kept at his Galveston mansion? Was the ghost of Lafitte's mistress still guarding his treasure? Before he gained his senses and opened his eyes—she had disappeared! Needless to say, the man from Humble wasted no time either, in leaving that spine-chilling spot.

Sometime after 1900, the Beazley house burned down from being struck by lightning, but the legend of ghosts and the treasure of Jean Lafitte still remains.

There is also a tale of ghosts and of a chest buried around the old Compton house on Red Bluff, but the lack of correlating facts make this story rather dubious.

The most credulous clue of all, however, came from a lady who resides in Kemah, who is supposed to be a direct descendant of Jean Lafitte himself. She admitted in the fall of 1964 that she had always heard that Lafitte's treasure was buried not far from the old Keller home in Seabrook. Do these heirs from Lafitte's pirate gang, who still live in the Clear Creek area, keep hoping to come across that much sought-after booty? Or will some lucky treasure hunter steal it away from right beneath their noses?

Some of Lafitte's men also left their own buried treasure that has yet to be found along the shores of Galveston Bay. One of these, a pirate named "Old Josie," was shipwrecked on the coast about 14 miles west of Sabine Pass on the Bolivar Peninsula in 1833. He and a crewman managed to salvage $40,000 of their ill-gotten gains and bury it ashore where they hoped to return later and claim it. Ten miles to the east they came upon John McGaffey's huge 17-room ranch house. McGaffey had built his house—the first one on the peninsula—in 1828, at the edge of Stamp's Pond just off the Bolivar trail. Here, the two shipwrecked sailors recuperated from their adventure and then made off for parts unknown.

In 1845, Josie returned to the ranch and told McGaffey about the hidden treasure. They both searched for it with a divining rod, but had no success and soon Old Josie left. McGaffey, however, afterwards spent his extra hours looking for the treasure and finally found it. He reburied the bulk, at a new location on his range, and then told his neighbors of his good fortune, also boasting of having buried another cache of more than $8,000 under his house. Shortly thereafter, when McGaffey was riding on the trail to New Orleans, he died suddenly, and the secret of the locations of his buried treasures died with him.

The old McGaffey ranch was recently acquired by the State of Texas Parks and Wildlife Department for use as a game area. Some lucky duck hunter, while digging for a blind, might one day strike his shovel on Old Josie's treasure chest, and find enough loot to keep him in shotgun shells forever.

A different sort of treasure was found on the old McGaffey land in the summer of 1970. The site of the lost Confederate Fort Manhasset was discovered three miles west of the McGaffey family cemetery alongside the road from Bolivar Point to Sabine Pass.

Fort Manhasset was built one month after the remarkable Battle of Sabine Pass in which Dick Dowling and 40 Confederates turned back 5,000 Federal troops and 20 ships on September 8, 1863. The new fort was to protect Fort Griffin, at Sabine Pass from a possible land attack from the west.

Major General J. B. Magruder ordered his chief engineer for east Texas, Major Getulius Kellersberger to design and construct the fort, which was completed about the middle of September. Five fortifications were built on the high ground that commanded the western beaches that stretched along the Bolivar peninsula: three redoubts that protected the western front were spaced 1800 feet apart, and two redans that comprised the eastern flank with the same equal spacing. All five fortifications were surrounded by earth embankments enforced with upright logs having sharpened ends.

The fort took its name from a Union coal schooner, the *USS Manhasset*, which beached and foundered about 1200 yards from the site while the fort was being built. Garrisoned with 266 men and 10 officers, the new fort had an armament of 6 large cannons and some brass howitzers. It was in operation until the end of the Civil War, when it was abandoned by the Confederates on May 20, 1865. For over one hundred years, Fort Manhasset was practically lost to history until the efforts of a modern-day treasure hunter led to its finding.

W. T. Block, an instructor of history at Lamar University, delved into an extensive research of several months until he was fairly certain that he knew where the fortifications were located; then with the aid of a bulldozer and some helpers enlisted from the Rebel Inn at Sabine Pass, he started digging into a small hillock on the north side of State Highway 87. Almost immediately, cannon balls began appearing in the freshly dug dirt, and after five more days of excavation the group found a total of 62 cannon balls of 24-pound and 32-pound sizes plus many grapeshot and shrapnel balls. A further finding of wood, square-nails and spikes, shoe soles, bones, black powder, and a cannon elevating screw assured the exploratory group that they had definitely located the abandoned fort site.

Although no cannons were found, researcher Block is convinced that the brass howitzers—highly treasured by Civil War collectors—are still buried somewhere among the remains of old Fort Manhasset.

But the prize that captures the imagination of most treasure hunters is yet to be found. . . .the treasure chests of pirate Jean Lafitte. Certainly, some of the most promising areas to search for such a treasure, would be around Lafitte's old fort, or near the dwelling sites of any of his cohorts who later lived on Galveston Island after its abandonment by the pirate commune.

Stephen Churchill—one of Lafitte's most trusted lieutenants—was the first settler on the island at the deserted pirate village after it was abandoned. In 1827, he lived at what was termed his "Diggins"; located northeast of the corner of Water Street (Avenue A.) and Eleventh Street, near the Galveston wharves. Around his dwelling he planted several China trees and eventually became well-known in the community for that singular horticultural feat. Today, living memorials to this Galveston buccaneer can still be found in the form of the many China trees that grow around this spot where Stephen Churchill once lived.

A two-story brick custom-house was built by the Mexican government close by Churchill's "Diggins" and he was employed as a harbor pilot by the new Republic of Mexico, which had just gained independence from Spain. In 1837, the new Republic of Texas, which had just gained independence from Mexico, established a collector for the port of Galveston at the old Mexican custom-house. . . . He was none other than Gail Borden, Jr.—soldier, rancher, surveyor, newspaperman, printer, Galveston lot salesman, and inventor of the condensed milk process.

Borden shared the custom-house with Colonel Amasa Turner, a San Jacinto veteran, who had been appointed Post Commander of the Texas Army at Galveston. Colonel Turner related that two large China trees (planted by Churchill as part of his improvements) stood forty feet east of the old custom-house, and that Lafitte's old fort was on a high mound on the north side of Avenue A. three blocks west of that location.

The Mexican custom-house was later abandoned, and in 1840, Stephen Churchill petitioned the Galveston City Company for a deed to his "Diggins". Because of having been the first settler of the City of Galveston since Lafitte's time, he was so deeded Lot 14 in Block 730 of the plan of that city. Three blocks west of this tract, a State of Texas historical marker designates the site of Lafitte's old fort and home.

Would not one of Lafitte's most trusted lieutenants locate his "Diggins" close by where he might search for any treasure that his chief might have buried during his stay on Galveston Island? Perhaps he found some loot; if he did, he probably re-buried it, and so the area around Churchill's "Diggins" as well as the fortress stomping grounds of the buccaneer boss are certainly the most logical places to begin a hunt for the muchly sought-after treasure chests of Jean Lafitte.

Chapter Six

A Fortune to Be Found

Nine million dollars in gold is buried in a horseshoe-shaped lake somewhere close to Houston.

In 1899, Henry Barnes was working as a night steward in the old H. & T. C. Hospital in Houston. There was brought in a section hand named Palencio Garza, whose legs had been cut off by a railroad boxcar. Barnes was called in to tend this patient who was slowly dying from loss of blood. Upon hearing that he might die, the Mexican called Barnes to his side and told him that he had knowledge of a buried fortune which he wanted to pass on.

He said that his grandfather was a Spanish officer in charge of a caravan that was transporting 423 gold bars from Nacogdoches to San Antonio. Each gold bar weighed about 25 pounds. When the caravan was threatened by danger, the gold was buried and the trek continued on. Later, ill fate befell everyone but Garza's grandfather, who made a map drawn on goatskin, which he passed on to his family, hoping that someone might earn enough funds to go back and recover the gold.

Just before he died, Garza gave Barnes the name of his sister and handed him the map along with $160 in gold coins. The map showed the treasure site to be on a tongue of land running into a horseshoe-shaped lake. On this tongue of land was marked a big pine tree and the gold was shown buried . . . "so many feet toward the sun—from the tree."

Dr. Joe Stewart, who treated the Mexican at the hospital, helped Barnes search for such a lake for more than a year, but after having no luck, they gave up.

Barnes later owned an eating establishment, Barnes' Beanery, and in 1934 one of his customers was telling him about a good bull-frogging lake that was shaped like a horseshoe. This rang a gong in the back of Barnes' head as he had never been able to forget about the lost treasure on such a lake. He lost no time in enlisting the aid of some of his friends to help him look for the gold. This lake was called Fishhook Lake and was located on the south side of Spring Creek about three miles from the Rose Hill settlement.

After getting authority from Gus Bayer of Spring, Texas, who owned this lake, the expedition started out to recover the buried gold bars. Sure enough, there was a promontory on the lake that matched the one drawn on the goatskin map. There was no tree standing, as indicated on the map, but they did find the remains of a large pine stump—from which they measured the required distance and began digging.

Quite a deep shaft was sunk into the quicksand-like mud of the lake. One day, when a laborer stuck his shovel into the mud, there issued a terrible moan from the bottom of the hole . . . .just like a dying man's wail! The worker dropped his shovel, scrambled out of the hole and was never seen again. Nor was anything ever heard from Barnes or his crew about any gold being found in Fishhook Lake.

Others also must have heard of this lost treasure—for it was discovered that Dr. W. F. Dearen completely drained Deadman's Lake looking for the gold, and that in 1930, Clarence Sullivan and his brother carried on a treasure digging operation at the same lake that attracted over 2,000 curious spectators. The Sullivans charged the visitors a fee to watch the proceedings, and this was all the treasure the hunters collected. They found no other gold.

But did these prospectors find the right lake? There was nothing on the crudely drawn goatskin map to indicate the *location of the lake*—only the *location of the treasure with respect to the lake* was shown. The lake could be almost *any* horseshoe-shaped lake that might possibly be on a route from Nacogdoches to San Antonio.

One very large horseshoe lake that sticks out upon a cursory glance at the map of Harris County, lies across the Atascosita Road about three miles west of Lake Houston, and the area just northwest of Galveston Bay is dotted with many small hook-shaped lakes.

One such lake still remains the silent protector of 423 bars of gold worth $9,000,000!

It is a well-known fact that in the early thirties, a company of Mexican soldiers was carrying $600,000 on a trail between the San Jacinto River and the Brazos River. It was supposed that this group traveled on the Opelousas Road, but the way was not too clearly marked, and they could have taken any number of the primitive roads that existed in those days. Nevertheless, this troop was attacked by a band of Indians and they took refuge in the cover of a small grove of sweetgum trees.

While the attack ensued, some of the soldiers buried the gold somewhere in the grove of trees. It was not long until all the soldiers were killed—except one. He was so badly wounded that the Indians left him there dying. The soldier, however, managed to regain enough strength to travel until he reached help. He then told the story of the attack and of the buried gold just before he died. Everyone who heard of this story started searching for the grove of sweetgum trees and its treasure, but it was never found.

Many years later, some cowboys found a lot of arrowheads sticking into some sweetgum trees on Cypress Creek in the northern part of Harris County. Thinking that this might have been the site of the Indian battle, they set about digging up the earth around the grove, but no gold was found. Nearby residents continued to dig in this area, however no treasure was ever uncovered.

A German farmer found a Mexican silver dollar while cultivating around some trees on his farm, not far from Cypress. Supposing that the rest of the Mexican gold might be buried nearby, he completely dug up the remaining land around the grove. He found nothing else.

The familiar star-shaped leaf of a sweetgum tree might one day guide some lucky treasure hunter to a nice little fortune in Mexican gold, buried in the shade of its grove.

When the Mexican General Santa Anna was pursuing the Texas Army and government in 1836, he marched toward the little town of Harrisburg, on the banks of Buffalo Bayou. Hearing of his advance, all of the residents of this pioneer village fled in panic—some of them had time to bury their valuables, some did not. Santa Anna burned and looted what was left and then marched eastward to meet the Texas Army.

When his large force came to Sims Bayou and began its time-consuming water crossing, Santa Anna sent a scout ahead to determine the whereabouts of his enemy. The scout came back reporting that the Texans were some 25 miles away near Lynch's Crossing on the banks of Buffalo Bayou. A battle with them was most imminent.

It is very likely, as will be shown later, that the Mexican general knew that during the confusion of the coming battle, his loot and valuables as well as the army paychest might be stolen by thieves from among his own troops, or by the Texans. Thus, while the bulk of his army was concerned with crossing Sims Bayou, it would have been a wise move to take a small force and bury the gold nearby.

In April of 1899, an old Mexican came to Houston and

caused a lot of excitement when he claimed to be one of Santa Anna's personal bodyguards, and said that he knew where Santa Anna had buried a large cache of gold on the banks of Buffalo Bayou near Samuel Allen's house. He offered to share the gold with anyone who would help with financing an expedition to recover it. Most everyone knew that Samuel Allen's house was located on the bend of Buffalo Bayou close to where the Peden Company is now located near downtown Houston, and everyone knew that Santa Anna did not come that far inland on his trek across Texas. So no one was interested in investing any money in such a venture, and the old man was soon discouraged and went his way.

But what everyone did not know was that there was also a Sam Allen who owned a home on Buffalo Bayou *just east of Sims' Bayou,* right at the place where Santa Anna and his army had crossed. The Sinclair refinery now occupies this site. Could there really have been something to the old Mexican bodyguard's story?

Among those tanks of *black Texas gold*—could there be a buried treasure of *real Mexican gold*?

There is a legend that when Santa Anna arrived on the plains of Saint Hyacinth (San Jacinto), across from the camp of the Texan Army, he stuffed a cannon full of gold and plugged it up with sycamore branches. He then put the cannon aboard a small sailboat in order to prevent its capture during the coming battle. When the Texans sprang their surprise attack on the 21st of April, one of the guards scuttled the sailboat and set it adrift. It evidently sank somewhere around the vicinity of San Jacinto Bay, for it was never found.

"Uncle Chris" Casey, a native of Goose Creek, estimated that the cannon contained about $50,000 in gold. He believed that the sailboat sank at the mouth of Goose Creek.

After the battle at San Jacinto, General Santa Anna was

found alone some eight miles away from the battlefield on the banks of Vince's Bayou. When he was captured he was just a stone's throw from where Sam Allen's house was located. He had traveled almost in a straight line from his camp toward the place where his army had previously crossed at Sims' Bayou! He had no gun or supplies of any kind. Was he headed toward his cache of gold that the old bodyguard said was buried on the banks of the bayou? With such a fortune of gold as an ally, he might have thought that he could buy his way safely back to Mexico—but he was caught before he could get to it, if that was his plan. That old Mexican bodyguard might really have known where that gold was buried. It may still be there.

Santa Anna's campsite at San Jacinto is within full view of the location of another treasure worth $50,000. Directly to the east of this bivouac area, Peggy's Lake cuts a crescent into the mainland. On the high banks of this lake, Arthur McCormick built his home in the last months of 1824, and settled there with his wife Margaret and two sons. Somewhere around the house he buried his worldly fortune of gold since there were no banks nearby, thinking that he had done a smart thing, but his cleverness only went so far because, in 1827, he drowned while trying to cross Buffalo Bayou and he had failed to tell his family the location of the cache.

The widow McCormick, known to her neighbors as Aunt Peggy, never could find the hidden treasure, nor could her sons John and Michael. In 1854, the home burned, and Aunt Peggy burned with it. A summer residence was later built at the old McCormick place, and visitors to this new house were often entertained—and sometimes frightened—by ghostly sounds and lights, which the owner would explain "were simply the ghosts of Aunt Peggy and her two sons still trying to find the $50,000." One Houston banker, who was a guest, suffered such a scary experience that he swore never to set foot on the place at nighttime. This financier's love for fish, crabs and shrimp did not keep him entirely from visiting his bayshore friends, but

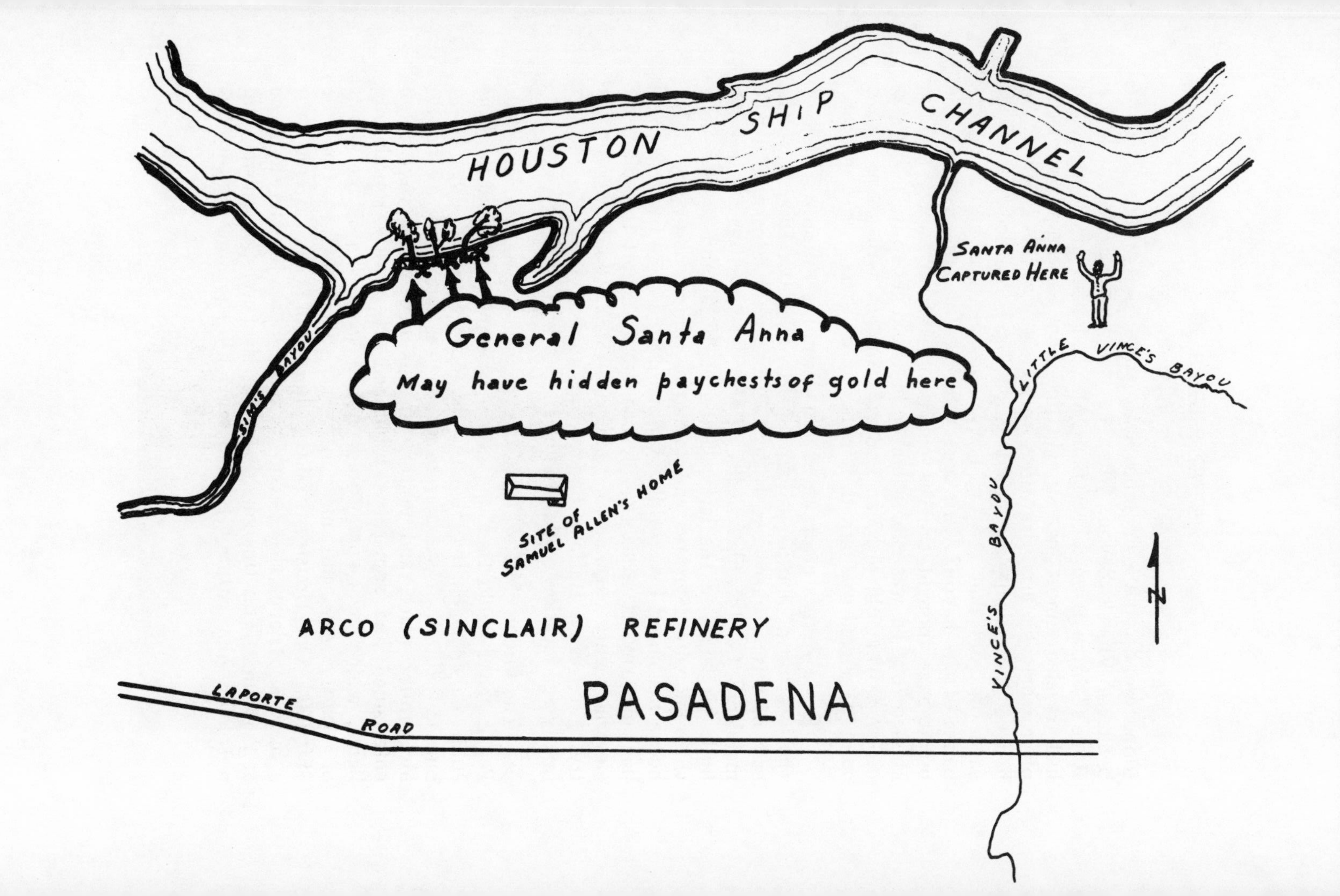

HOUSTON SHIP CHANNEL
SIM'S BAYOU
SANTA ANNA CAPTURED HERE
LITTLE VINCE'S BAYOU
General Santa Anna
May have hidden paychests of gold here
SITE OF SAMUEL ALLEN'S HOME
VINCE'S BAYOU
N
ARCO (SINCLAIR) REFINERY
LAPORTE ROAD
PASADENA

South bank of Buffalo Bayou near old Samuel Allen home—viewed from west bank of Sim's Bayou.

when evening shadows would fall, he would lose no time in leaving the premises.

Arthur McCormick's buried gold seems to be well protected.

The guns, sabers and equipment of the many hundreds of Mexican soldiers who were caught at Aunt Peggy's Gap during the Battle of San Jacinto still remain sunk in the mire of that deep 140-foot wide sluice. As these soldiers were trying to escape from the fierce charge of the Texans, they tried to cross this narrow outlet between Peggy's Lake and the bay, the depth was deceiving and so by the hundreds they wallowed and sank as the Texans pushed them back. Their heavy equipment pulled them under and the mud of Aunt Peggy's Gap claimed their lives forever. The armory that these soldiers carried—a real prize for arms collectors—still lies buried deep beneath the surface of this ignominious gap, waiting to be recovered.

Immediately after the battle, Robert H. Hunter and several other Texas soldiers probed this same lagoon with long poles, in search of Santa Anna's pay chest which they had heard had been thrown there, but could only feel the bodies of dead men and horses. If a pay chest actually was thrown in that morass, a more careful probing and the use of a discriminator-type metal detector from a small boat would make this one of the easiest treasures to find. Since this location is in a State of Texas Park (San Jacinto Battleground) close adherence to the Antiquities Law should be followed if anyone seeks this particular treasure.

The Texans had two pieces of artillery that they used with great effect during that battle. These were two cannons that were given to the Texas Army by the citizens of Cincinnati, Ohio. They were affectionately known by the soldiers as the "Twin Sisters." After the battle they were placed on the northwest side of the market square in Houston and were fired on the 21st of every April to celebrate the anniversary date of that Texas victory. During the Civil War, they were taken for use by the Confederate Army.

No one knows exactly what happened to the famed "Twin Sisters" after the cessation of that war.

Many people think that the two cannons flanking the main door of the State Capitol building at Austin are the "Twin Sisters," but those two pieces were given to the Republic of Texas by General T. J. Chambers and were made of iron. Dr. S. O. Young, who remembered seeing them many times in Houston, insisted that the "Twin Sisters" were made of brass and that many other native Houstonians, including Colonel William Stafford, I. C. Lord, Owen Cochran, and Henry Thompson could vouch for that fact. Whether made of iron or brass, the historical significance of the two cannons is so great that they present a treasure worth looking for.

When the Federal forces captured Galveston in 1863, the "Twin Sisters" were said to have been taken there and used by the Confederate Army during the Battle of Galveston. This was the last time they were known to have been used. At one time, however, they were reported to be in the National Museum at Washington; another report has them sunk in the mud flats of Galveston Bay to prevent their capture by the Yankee troops; yet another story seems to be the most believable account of their disappearance:

At the cessation of the Civil War in 1865, Dr. H. N. Graves was being transported on a troop train from the Confederate camp in Galveston. When the train arrived at the Galveston Houston and Henderson depot in Harrisburg, he noticed many cannons that were dumped along the side of the railroad track. They had probably been taken from the forts at Galveston and were being made ready for shipment to the North. Two of the cannons in particular caught his eye. They were the "Twin Sisters". There was no doubt that the cannons would be put to use by the victorious Union Army. Sentimental pride prevailed upon Graves to do something to keep these two prized emblems of Texas freedom out of the hands of the Yankee troops.

He enlisted the aid of several sympathetic messmates—Sol Thomas, Ira Pruitt, Jack Taylor and John Barnett, to steal the cannons away from the depot. With the help of his Negro servant Dan, this group rolled the cannons to the bayou, where they took off the carriages and sank them; they then rolled the barrels about 400 yards into the woods, and buried them in a shallow grave only two or three feet deep. Several of the trees nearby were marked, so that they would be able to find the spot later. Each one of this furtive group was sworn never to reveal the secret burial place of the "Twin Sisters" until all the threat of enemy confiscation was passed.

Later in 1905, John Barnett and Dr. Graves determined that it was time to recover the beloved cannons. They journeyed back to Harrisburg, but the geography and landmarks had changed so much over the past years, that they were unable to find the spot where they had buried the barrels. Dr. Graves later returned to the depot in 1920, but could create no interest in securing help to search for the site. Thus the resting place of the famous "Twin Sisters" still remains lost and the two cannons lie silently . . . an unfound prize for some lucky treasure hunter.

It is said that the first shot of the Texas Revolution was fired in the Galveston Bay area. When William Barret Travis and several other Texas colonists were imprisoned in the Mexican fort at Anahuac in the summer of 1832, angry Texans advanced in arms on the fort. Two of these, William J. Russell and Ritson "Jawbone" Morris, crawled to within 40 yards of the garrison and opened fire upon the guards, killing one and wounding several others. This was no doubt the first violent action taken in the Texian's War for Independence. Thus, the site of the old fort at Anahuac might hold many interesting buried relics which would be highly treasured by those who love the lore of Texas history. The brick remains of that historical fort can still be seen on the edge of the east bank of the Trinity River in the public park at Anahuac.

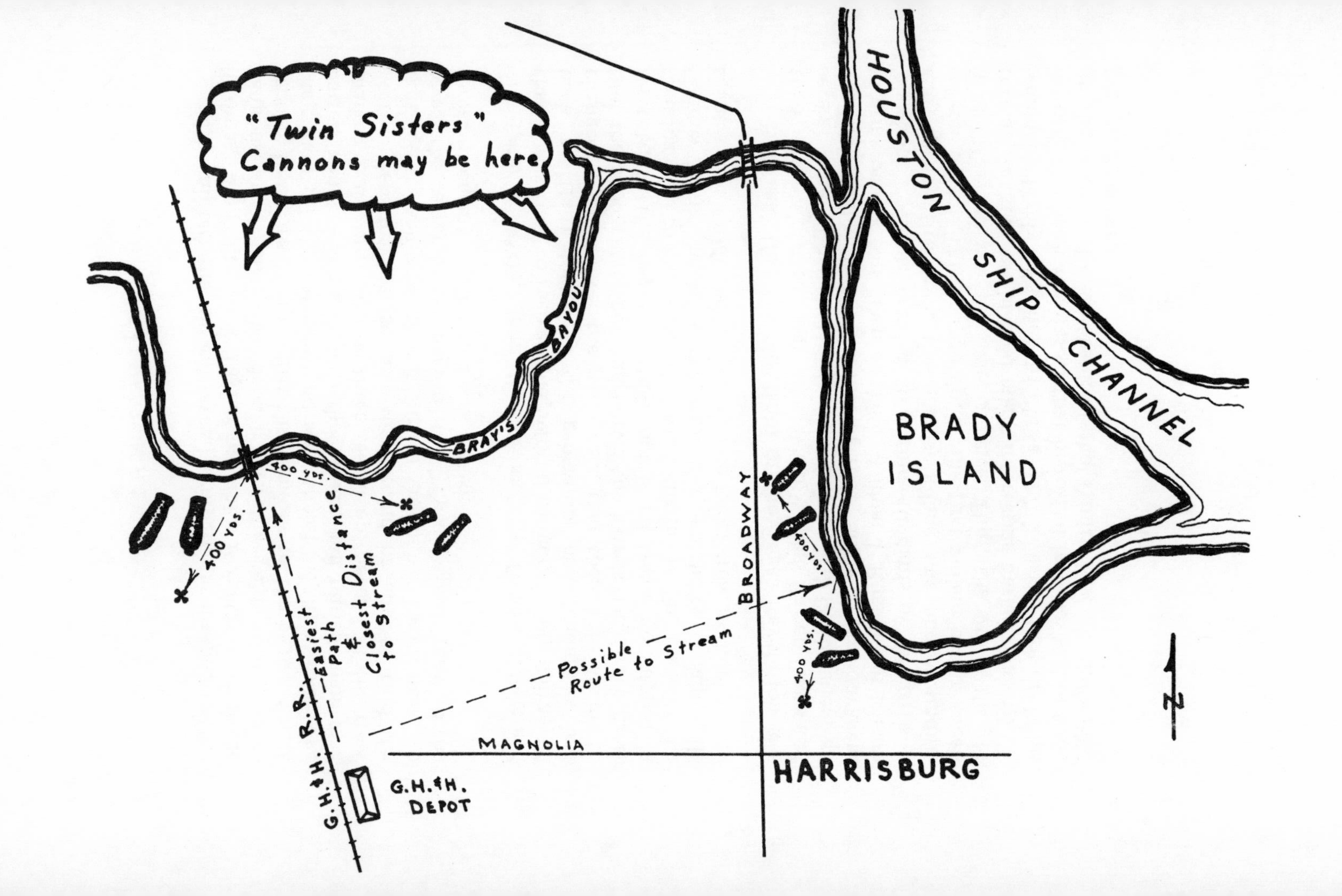

"Twin Sisters" Cannons may be here
BRAY'S BAYOU
HOUSTON SHIP CHANNEL
BRADY ISLAND
G.H.&H. R.R.
Easiest Path & Closest Distance to Stream
400 YDS.
400 YDS.
BROADWAY
Possible Route to Stream
400 YDS.
400 YDS.
MAGNOLIA
HARRISBURG
G.H.&H. DEPOT
N

Excavation of Fort Anahuac in 1968 by the Southwestern Historical Exploration Society—instigated and directed by the author.

About half a mile north of these ruins on the same side of the river, near the home of Mrs. Mary Mull, is the site of old Confederate Fort Chambers. Civil war relic-hunters might find quite a few items of interest in the area around this old fort.

Not far from this site, near a lagoon north of Wallisville, on the east bank of the Trinity River, there is a treasure site of another kind . . . an abandoned Spanish mission! The mission Nuestra Senora de la Luz and its fort San Augustin de Ahumada, were built in 1755 to protect 50 Spanish families and bring the Word of God to the neighboring Orcoquisac Indians. Malaria, mosquitoes, and unfriendly Indians forced the Franciscan friars to abandon the mission in 1772. What ancient treasures of early Texas history must still be buried around the vicinity of this Spanish ghost mission?

There are even some antiquities from the American Revolution which might be found on Galveston Isle, for in the same year that the Spanish mission was abandoned, Cavalier Gremer and sixty seamen were shipwrecked upon the island. Then known as Isla Culebra (Snake Island) from the many rattlesnakes that infested the bleak sandy shores, the island claimed their ship and its cargo that it was carrying between Vera Cruz and New Orleans. This cargo was to have been used by the Spaniards who, through the influence of Benardo de Galvez, had joined France in aiding the American colonists in their revolt against the Crown.

The Karankawa Indians gave Gremer and his companions so much trouble that they escaped from the island making no effort to recover their precious cargo; hence those lost artifacts of the American Revolution are still waiting for discovery by some lucky Galveston Islander.

Chapter Seven

Conquistadors and Indians

Gold is not the only treasure buried around the Galveston Bay area. There are many artifacts of antiquity that are worth more than their weight in gold to the collector or historian. Indian relics for instance. The coastal Indians depended very heavily upon the harvest of the sea for their food, and since the easiest to obtain were shellfish—clams, oysters, crabs or shrimp—their abandoned campsites, or middens, are easy to find. Simply spot a deposit of shucked shells on any high place along the bayshore, and you will most likely find that it is the garbage leavings of an aboriginal tribe; their campsite will be at the same location.

Many of these sites can be found along the high banks of San Jacinto Bay, Peggy Lake and Black Duck Bay in the vicinity of the old McCormick place. Nearly all of the bayous and streams that empty into Galveston bay have their banks spotted with these tell-tale shell deposits of Indian campgrounds. Old and Lost River, Taylor's Bayou, Trinity River, Buffalo Bayou, Cut-off Bayou, Middle or Armand Bayou, Little Cedar Creek, Dickinson's Bayou, Keith's Lake, Cedar Bayou and the San Jacinto River all may be easily traveled by boat from which such clam-shell mounds can be seen.

The shores of Clear Lake abound with Indian campsites as do the banks of Clear Creek. As far up the creek as three miles southwest of Webster, C. L. Sweet found middens full of charcoal, flint chips, pottery shards and discarded arrowheads. A beautiful serrated spear-point was found by Mrs. Doris Miller about two blocks from Galveston Bay in the dirt that was spilled out of the draglines when the Houston Lighting and Power Company spillway was dug between Baycliff and San Leon; pieces of pottery were found in the vicinity of Moses Lake by Mrs. Robert Scott of Dickinson.

Robert Hancock Hunter, who settled at Morgan's Point in 1822, related how a large band of Cronks lived on the shore of Galveston Bay at Little Cedar Creek, and would entice unsuspecting white colonists crossing the bay by waving a white flag. The colonists, seeing the flag, supposed that someone was in trouble and would sail in to land ashore, only to be captured by the Indians, killed and eaten. Hunter remembers being in a scouting party that crept up close to the Indian encampment and seeing the cannibals finishing off the hands and feet of some early white Texans. The enraged scouting group promptly attacked the camp and made quick restitution for that horrible act. The Cronks, however, continued to stay at this campsite for many years, and so the area around Little Cedar Creek would be an excellent spot to look for Indian artifacts.

A Karankawa Indian burial ground was found several miles west of Lafitte's Grove, where a bloody battle took place between the pirates and the Indians. These Indians also lived around Lynchburg and along the lower Trinity River; oftentimes making their summer camps on Red Fish Bar and around Red Bluff.

On the small island at the mouth of Clear Creek—made when the channel was cut from Clear Creek to Galveston Bay through the peninsula that is now Kemah—a huge deposit of clamshells remains. These shells were once part of a much larger shellbank made by the Indians on the tip of the highly elevated point. So great was this deposit, that a railroad track was run out to the point and the shell carried by trains to make the base for the railroad track that runs from LaPorte to Galveston. To find Indian artifacts, all one has to do is to walk along that track and examine the clamshell base under the rails.

GALVESTON BAY

When the clamshell deposit was mostly removed from the Kemah peninsula, a channel was cut through it and a small low-lying island was left. Here, in 1939, Tony Muecke found some arrowheads and shards around a grove of hackberry trees that had grown up in its backwater cove. Indian artifacts may still be found on this last vestige of that once popular high bluff called Kemah—an Indian word for "where the winds blow".

In searching for Indian artifacts in this area, it is possible to find objects of antiquity used by some of conquistador Narvaez's men who were shipwrecked upon Galveston Island in 1528. One of these, Cabeza de Vaca, related how eighty of his shipmates were cast upon the island and took refuge there with a band of Indians. Although accidental, this actually became the first settlement of Europeans on the North American continent—a fact that has been overlooked by historians, up to this date.

This conquistador group befriended the Indians by giving them hawk-bells and beads and acting as physicians for their sick. Cabeza de Vaca stayed on the mainland at various Indian encampments around the shores of Galveston Bay for six years, before finally trecking back to Mexico City. The metal hawk-bells and other relics left by these conquistadors with the Indians of Galveston Bay are some of the most important unfound treasures of American history.

THE PIRATE "ALABAMA."

THE picture of this famous pirate, which will be found on the preceding page, has been attentively examined by Captain Hagar of the *Brilliant*, and pronounced correct. He has kindly given us the following certificate of the fact:

I have seen the drawing of the *Alabama* which will appear in the next number of *Harper's Weekly*, and pronounce it a correct picture.

GEORGE HAGAR, Capt. of ship *Brilliant*.

October 18, 1862.

No ship should sail out of port without this number of *Harper's Weekly*, in order that her captain may be able to recognize the pirate.

HARPER'S WEEKLY.

SATURDAY, NOVEMBER 1, 1862.

This drawing appeared on the front page of Harper's Weekly, *November 1, 1862, more than two months before the fateful encounter of the* Hatteras *with the* Alabama *off Galveston, January 11, 1863. The warning at right was the lead item on the weekly's editorial page.*

THE PIRATE "ALABAMA," *ALIAS* "290," CERTIFIED TO BE CORRECT BY CAPTAIN HAGAR OF THE "BRILLIANT."

Courtesy of *Rice University Review*

Chapter Eight

Civil War Treasure

The Galveston Bay area has many treasures to be found by those who value and collect Civil War relics. The Federal warship *Hatteras*, for example, was sunk just offshore of Galveston Island during a running battle with the famed Confederate steamer *Alabama* on January 11, 1863. The first edition of this book, in 1966, pointed out that the armament and cargo of this vessel were valuable and had never been recovered. Almost ten years later, some enterprising treasure hunters found the *Hatteras*, and Dr. Frank Vandiver, notable Civil War historian at Rice University, declared that the find was very significant and should produce many important relics.

For four years, Dr. Paul A. Cloutier, Charles Rose, and Jeff Burke searched for the *Hatteras.* Using a magnetometer towed behind Rose's yacht *Sanray*, they eventually located a sunken wreck on January 18, 1976, approximately twenty miles south of the Galveston jetties at the position indicated as the *Hatteras* on the map that was available with the first issue of this book. Diving upon this wreck, these modern-day discoverers found irrefutable evidence of it being the long lost *Hatteras*. All that remains now, is to recover the centuries-old artifacts, thanks to the efforts of Cloutier and his crew.

Dry land relic-hunting is much easier. Regard the fact that the Confederate Army maintained a fort at the entrance to Goose Creek. It was built on the high bluff of the peninsula between Black Duck Bay and the north shore of Goose Creek so that it could command a view of Buffalo Bayou, Black Duck

Bay, Goose Creek, San Jacinto Bay and the upper reaches of Galveston Bay. Although this site is covered with dense underbrush, it would be an excellent place to explore for mementos of the Civil War. Other Confederate forts were also built at Virginia Point, Pelican Island, San Leon, Bolivar Point, and on Galveston Island near the ferry landing, on the Gulf beach, and on both sides of the causeway to the mainland.

On the 17th of November, in 1956, a Parker Bros. shell dredge was operating in Trinity Bay about three miles northwest of Smith's Point. The bit was cutting some 20 feet deep into a shelf of oyster shell, when suddenly, hunks of oak timbers started showing up on the shell piled up on the barge alongside; next appeared a revolver, a leather holster, some coal, a pipe, two axes, a grappling hook, some pieces of bone and a nickel plated pressure guage made in 1857. The captain then realized that the dredge might be destroying something of historical value, and he stopped the dredging and marked the spot with a yellow can bouy. The relics retrieved were obviously of Civil War vintage, and it was concluded that this sunken ship was possibly the Union flagship *Westfield* that had gone down with all hands during the Battle of Galveston on New Year's Day in 1863.

In the fall of 1862, the Union forces had captured the city of Galveston and manned six large gunboats to blockade the port. This blockade created a vital shortage of provisions and supplies at the town of Houston. The people there had to improvise with various things in order to subsist; some even resorted to making coffee out of ground-up dried okra. The situation became so unbearable, that a group of Houstonians conspired to float four small steamboats from Houston, down Buffalo Bayou to meet the Union fleet at Galveston in battle. The decks of these four craft were lined with cotton bales for protection and to disguise them to look like ordinary merchant ships.

Choosing New Year's Day as an unlikely time to do battle,

sharpshooting rebel marines concealed themselves behind the cotton bales, drifted innocently down the bayou into Galveston harbor and took the Yankee fleet by surprise. After a short but bloody fight, these four "cottonclads" defeated the entire Union Navy in the Galveston waters.

The Confederate steamer *Neptune* was sunk in the channel, and the Union flagship of eight large guns, the *Westfield* had run aground, after being put out of commission by the sharpshooting rebels. The Union commander, William B. Renshaw, seeing that the battle was going the wrong way, set about to destroy his flagship so that it would not fall into the hands of his enemy. In doing so, the ship accidentally exploded before the Commodore and his crew could get off. All hands were lost.

The sunken wreck of the *Westfield* remained on a bar just off Pelican Island for many years, but disappeared after a bad storm in 1886. It is entirely possible that the remains of the wreck floated off the bar from the high tide and winds, and were carried into Trinity Bay and finally sank, to be found in later years by the shell dredge.

The fact that the *Westfield* was a commodore's flagship, makes it probable that there would be many valuable relics to be retrieved from its wreckage. The eight large cannons themselves would be worth close to their weight in gold to a Civil War arms collector.

One attempt was made to explore the sunken ship, as soon as the discovery by the dredge was announced. That November, the yacht *Marsha Ann* anchored above the sunken ship, and divers, supervised by Dr. Nils Muensch, braved the icy cold winter waters to uncover the secret of the wreck. The water was surprisingly clear, but the movement of the divers disturbed the dredged silt and muddied the area so much that nothing could be seen. The divers could only explore by feeling around with probes. After retrieving several oak pegged timbers from the wreck, it was decided that the twenty-foot deep ledge might cave in on a diver probing blindly below. The situation was too hazardous for further exploration; so the expedition gave up. This sunken wreckage of history and its cargo of artifacts still lies unrecovered at the bottom of Trinity Bay.

Four million dollars in gold lies hidden, a little farther north, along the banks of the Trinity River.

In 1832, a cousin of George Washington, Col. Hamilton Washington, sold his huge Virginia plantation and moved to Texas, bringing with him fifty of his best slaves. After staying a while with a relative, John Beazley at LaPorte, he bought a large tract of land on the banks of the Trinity River, where he started quite a prodigious farming operation. Four miles east of where Highway 59 now crosses the river at Urbana, he constructed a large plantation home, which he called his "Big House." This great house was located on the river bank where the Trinity divides Polk and San Jacinto Counties.

Col. Washington was a bachelor who cut an imposing figure as he was six feet tall, weighed 200 pounds and was every bit the ruler of all he surveyed. He was over 70 years old at the time of the Civil War and grew very apprehensive that the Union troops might soon come upon his fine plantation and loot his belongings. In the middle of the night, the colonel woke up three of his most trusted slaves and told them to get some horses and shovels ready. He then led the slaves to a room in the "Big House" where a huge iron pot was sitting in the middle of the floor. The pot was filled to the brim with gold coins. The colonel instructed the slaves to carry the heavy pot out and sling it between the horses, so that it could be carried a good distance. When this was done, the colonel blindfolded the slaves and led them and the horses laden with the pot of gold out into the night.

Soon they came to a spot along the banks of the river where the colonel had the slaves dig a trench and bury the pot of gold. This strange procession then returned to the "Big

House," and Col. Washington slept soundly that night, comforted by the thought that his gold was safe from falling into the hands of any marauding Yankee soldiers.

This was the beginning of a mammoth treasure hunt, for his slaves, no matter how trustworthy, could not keep such a secret; soon everyone knew about the buried gold and many tried to find it. The old colonel continually checked to see if his fortune was safe. But only at night. So that no one could track or follow him, the colonel resorted to a very clever tactic—he nailed an extra set of heels to the toes of his boots—so that no gold hunter could tell if he were coming or going. A descendant of one of his slaves, who lives at Urbana, still has one of the colonel's amazing two-heeled boots.

This ruse must have worked, for, after the war, the colonel still kept his treasure buried for safekeeping. Suddenly, in 1868, he died. It was thought that he might have been poisoned; but no matter how he expired, the secret of the location of his gold went with him.

Before his death, the colonel had told others that his cache consisted of $135,000 in gold (now worth over $4,000,000), but he told no one of its location. Everyone in the vicinity searched for this lost treasure, but nothing was ever found. One of the slaves who had helped bury the gold remembered that he had heard the bleating of goats close by the spot where the pot was buried. When old-time residents recalled that some goat pens were located at the fishing camp of J. L. Robbins near Drew's landing, the area was soon pock-marked with holes left by eager treasure hunters trying to find Col. Washington's gold; they also had no luck.

It still has not been found. Somewhere on the banks of the Trinity River lies a fortune . . . an iron pot and $4,000,000 in gold.

Chapter Nine

A Storehouse of Relics

Galveston Bay is connected to the metropolitan city of Houston by a sluggish stream called Buffalo Bayou that has silently kept guard over an impressive collection of Civil War relics for over one hundred years.

Buffalo Bayou has always been a center of action since the day a couple of New York brothers named Allen first staked out a red-flagged subdivison on its banks and called it Houston. From the beginning, this stream was the lifeblood of the new community. It would bring its early settlers to Texas by boat and eventually turn into a water highway that would enable the young city to become a leading port of the world.

The first Texans were visibly impressed by the tranquil beauty of the Bayou. Fish teemed beneath its crystal clear waters and the fragrance of magnolia blossoms belied the danger of alligators that sometimes lurked behind the garden-like vegetation that overhung the banks. Trout, redfish, flounder and porpoise were seen as far up as the new settlement of Houston, and perch, buffalo, catfish and gar abounded in the waters that were farther upstream. In earlier times, these fish helped to sustain the Arkokisa Indians as they guided their canoes up the bayou in search of bison, and as a result of these aboriginal hunting parties, the Spaniards called the stream Rio Cibolo—Buffalo River. When Stephen F. Austin drew his first map of Texas in 1822, he labeled the river as "Rio Cibolo," but later publications of his map translated this name to "Buffalo Bayou" and Texas colonists soon adopted that usage.

With the coming of civilization, the bayou's beauty quickly vanished. The crystal clear waters became muddied with the silty runoff of drainage canals, the fish died from pollution and the magnolia trees fell as victims to the woodsmen's axes as the early pioneers began settling along its banks.

From where the bayou's waters emptied into Galveston Bay to the site of the new town of Houston, many settlements and proposed cities were started along the winding stream—towns such as New Washington, Scottsburg, Crockett, Lynchburg, San Jacinto, Buffalo or Pokersville, Louisville, Hamilton, Harrisburg, Tallowtown, Frosttown, and Beauchampville. These soon failed, however, and were abandoned or swallowed up by the more popular city of Houston.

This thriving new city began using the bayou to a great advantage for its embryonic commerce; even the neighboring Indian tribes used its banks to camp on and trade with the settlers at the Preston Street bayou crossing, while the traffic of ships—both steam and sail—brought people, animals, food and supplies to hurry the building of a metropolis. But in the middle of the nineteenth century, the frantic pace of the burgeoning city came to a sudden stop. The Civil War had come to Texas and the resultant Federal blockade of the Gulf ports caused an immediate cessation of commerce.

In the ending months of 1862, the Union blockade along the Texas coast grew tighter. Supply lines to Houston were cut off, and as food and munitions were no longer available by boat, businesses suffered and failed, people starved, and the Confederacy became weakened by the disarming of its arsenals at Houston.

This impasse was soon solved by the audacious courage of Rebel blockade-runners—skilled ship captains who would load their crafts with cotton at Houston, sneak down the bayou during the day, and at nighttime secretly maneuver their way past the patrolling Union gunboats that guarded the entrance of

Galveston Bay. The cotton found its sale in England, and British munitions and supplies found their way to the Confederacy aboard the returning blockade-running ships as their crafty masters would again slip through the Union blockade and make their way up Buffalo Bayou to Houston. At the foot of Caroline, San Jacinto, Milam and Main Streets, the ships would tie up and unload their cargo. The munitions would then be carted to the Confederate arsenals that existed near the Caroline Street dock and around the John Kennedy trading post building on Market Square.

As a means to defend the city against a Federal attack, an earthen fort was built on the north side of the Bayou opposite the landing dock at Main Street, known as Allen's Landing. After the fort was built, however, the Confederate officers in charge found out that its location across the Bayou from the city proper was too inconvenient for the troops quartered in the town, and that supply lines from the arsenals could be too easily cut off if the Union forces attacked by coming up the Bayou. Consequently, the fort was abandoned, and the citizenry of Houston laughingly referred to it as "Fort Humbug" or "Fort Blunder." It later found use as a prison for Union soldiers captured at the Battle of Galveston in 1863.

As the war progressed, one Confederate ship, heavily laden with munitions, successfully escaped through the Union blockade, but had developed such a bad leak that it was in danger of sinking. It was towed to the foot of Milam Street in order to discharge its cargo; however, the leaking became so severe that the ship sank before its complete load of arms and ammunition could be taken on shore, and for some unknown reason, the Confederacy abandoned the ship and its cargo to the depths of the Bayou.

At the cessation of the Civil War, the munitions of this sunken blockade-runner were joined by more Confederate ordnance as the arsenals in Houston disposed of their explosive cannon projectiles by dumping them into Buffalo Bayou. Consequently, at the foot of Milam and adjoining downtown Houston streets, cannon balls have often been found in the bayou and along its banks.

In the years that ensued after the Civil War, the sunken blockade-runner could be seen at various times when the waters of the Bayou were at an extremely low ebb. Dr. Ebb N. Gray remembered looking down from the Milam Street bridge, seeing the ship and the munitions that lay with it and wondering where the ship came from. Curious and venturesome boys would often dive down to the ship and retrieve cannon balls. Some of these projectiles were loaded with black powder and after drying out would explode if tampered with wrongly. Such incidents caused several deaths and quite an amount of property damage to early Houstonians.

In 1908, a blustery norther blew most of the water out of Buffalo Bayou, and the ship could be seen very plainly. Felix Richard recalled seeing a small cannon about five feet long still affixed to its foredeck. He remembered examining rifle boxes on board that were inscribed with foreign writing (the Confederacy imported flintlock rifles from Austria and converted them to faster-firing more reliable percussionlock weapons at the Texas towns of Anderson, Plentitude, Rusk, Bastrop and Tyler). He also saw many boxes of cannon projectiles which he described as "large bottles with brass-screwed tops" (these were evidently the imported British Blakely shells which employed intricate brass fuses on their fore-ends which closely resembled bottle tops). Taking one of these projectiles off the boat, he kept it as a souvenir for many years, but after learning of its danger of exploding, buried it in his backyard.

The same year, another adventurous youth, John Gresham, accompanied his grandfather to the Bayou and took a rifle, a saber, and forty round cannonballs off of the sunken ship. He used a small wagon to carry the relics home where his mother immediately demanded that he get rid of the dangerous objects.

Nearby, a concrete sidewalk was being poured in front of the Mock Gun Shop, and young Gresham gave his cannon balls to the concrete finishers who placed them in the wet cement to make a border decoration on the walk. These balls were explosive, and were later taken up by a demolition squad and destroyed. Round cavities left in the concrete by these balls can yet be seen at 1012 McGowen Street, and still buried in the doorway of the building there are several solid grapeshot that form the word "MOCK"—a silent reminder of days gone by.

A young man in 1910, W. L. Cleveland was employed as an oyster-shucker on the wharf between the Milam Bridge and Travis Street. He recalled seeing some men diving on the sunken blockade-runner and recovering several boxes full of rifles. For some unknown reason, the ship was then blown up and its planks and timbers drifted down the Bayou past the pier upon which he was working. The relics of the Confederacy that had not been taken from the old ship were once again doomed to the depths of Buffalo Bayou.

When the Milam Street bridge was rebuilt in 1947, over three hundred cannon balls were pulled out of the Bayou by the construction draglines, and the explosive balls disposed of by demolition experts at Fort Sam Houston.

Following information given in the first edition of this book, the Southwestern Historical Exploration Society located the site of the sunken blockade-runner in the summer of 1968, and recovered a wealth of artifacts from the Bayou. Using an eighty-ton dragline and digging into about five feet of the muddy bottom at the center of the stream approximately ten feet downstream from the Milam Bridge, bucket-loads of mud and debris were washed and carefully sifted by Society members. After two days, the operation ceased and the Society took stock of its findings.

Lost from sight for over a century, the following Civil War relics had been recovered from beneath the water of Buffalo

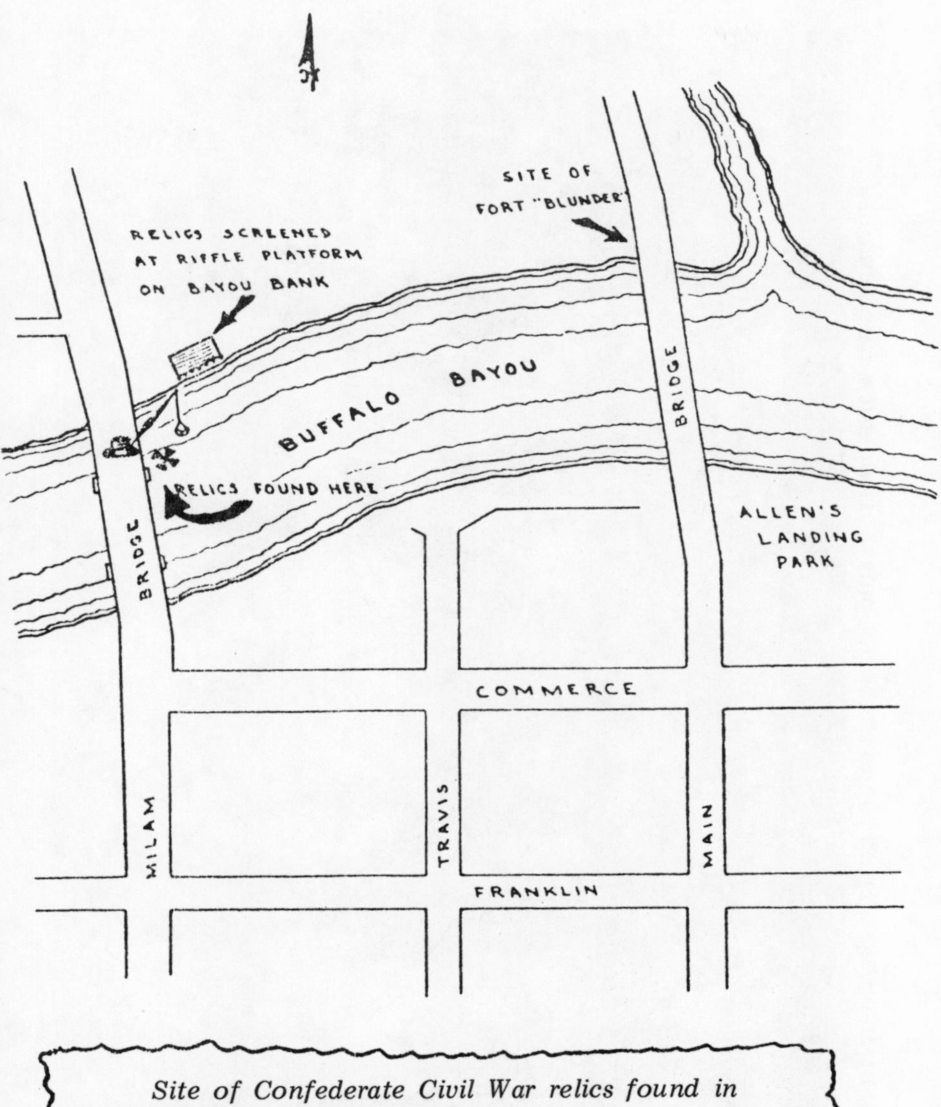

Site of Confederate Civil War relics found in downtown Houston.

Recovering Civil War relics from mud and debris out of Buffalo Bayou in Houston.

Bayou in downtown Houston: Explosive cannon projectiles, round cannon balls, minie balls, brass nipple fuses, canister complete with ball load, numerous grape shot, pistol balls, rifle balls, musket and/or shrapnel balls, friction primer, enfield bayonet, musket wrench, rifle barrel, belaying pin, brass military buttons, horseshoes, knives, square nails, spikes, chest locks, keys, old bottles and coins. It was concluded by Society members that many more historical objects still lie on the bottom of the Bayou at that spot waiting to be raised at a later date.

Chapter Ten

Paper Profits

There is another horde of treasure that exists around Galveston Bay which has been grossly overlooked. . . . historical papers. Sometimes called "rare documents", these papers consist of original old writings relating to historical persons, places or events; the older the writings, the more famous the persons or events, the more valuable the documents become.

Included in this category are maps, letters, journals, diaries, notes, books, drawings, surveys and legal instruments. The discovery of any one of these old papers will usually present a handsome profit to its finder.

Rare documents turn up at the most unexpected times. During World War II, a protracted artillery dual between the Germans and General Patton's American task force, reduced the French seacoast town of Saint Malo to ruins. Famous for having been a haven and retirement place for the buccaneers and corsairs of earlier times, Saint Malo suffered the fate of seeing almost all of its historical edifices and venerable monuments destroyed in that engagement.

In 1945, while cleaning out the rubble of war amidst the old historical section of Saint Malo, a citizen named Yves Hémar found three old copy-books in a trunk in the cellar under a collapsed house. Eaten by rats, charred by fire, and wet with rain, the old copy-books were carefully restored to readability and found to be a series of memoirs written by a 17th Century French buccaneer, who sailed for "the American islands" as a young man and returned to Saint Malo many years later enriched by his plundered booty.

These memoirs were translated into English, edited, and published in 1954 as *The Memoirs of a Buccaneer*; being a first-hand account of the adventures and amours of Louis Le Golif, better known by his nickname *Borgnefesse* (meaning "one-buttock" or "half-bottom") because of having lost the fleshy part of his left buttock in one of his first sea battles. The finder of those charred manuscripts, among the ruins of Saint Malo, thus profited both himself and the many readers who have enjoyed that most colorful and humorous account of life aboard the pirate seas.

Digging must be done to uncover a rare document. Not digging of an earthy kind but digging into the attics of old houses; digging in trunks and drawers of antique furniture; digging into crates and boxes used for storage; digging into files and map records of old business establishments; digging into the forgotten corners of lock cabinets, safes and deposit boxes; digging in the walls, nooks and crannies of old or abandoned houses; digging into any area where someone in the past may have hidden or stored a document which was valuable then, and which might be considerably more valuable today.

One such digger into the past is an antique dealer from Galveston, who became so enamoured with rare documents that he now devotes most of his time in hunting for them. Collecting over 5,000 items pertaining to the early Galveston era, he has made great use out of examining existing historical texts to find clues that point to the location of rare documents, some of which have profited him considerably.

For instance, in 1971, he found an original 1836 land grant to the east end of Galveston Island that has netted him offers of up to $10,000 from institutions and collectors. The grant was given by Texas President *ad interim*, David G. Burnet, to William Fairfax Gray and Robert Triplett according to Gray's published diary; yet, due to lack of other evidence, most historians tended to disbelieve its existence. This collector was convinced, however, that Gray's diary observations were generally accurate, and began a campaign of sleuthing among the Triplett and Gray heirs that eventually turned up the valuable document.

The value of such historical papers is further proven by the sum of $15,000 that he was paid for only a portion of his collection of manuscripts concerning early Texan Samuel May Williams, secretary to Stephen F. Austin and one of the founders of the City of Galveston.

Some of the most interesting documents to make their appearance in recent years, are the Lafitte Papers—a Lafitte family collection of letters, notes, memoirs, documents, journals, tin-types, photographs, daguerreotypes, and Bibles containing genealogical information—which, for the first time, in 1977, were made available to the general public at the Sam Houston Regional Library and Research Center of Liberty, Texas.

The Lafitte Papers answer many questions about the unknown part of the life of Jean Lafitte. Historians have long disputed the birthplace of the famous corsair, placing it variously at New York, Bordeaux, St. Malo or Bayonne, France. . . . the Papers reveal that Lafitte was born at Port au Prince, Haiti on April 22, 1782.

History has also failed to explain exactly what happened to the pirate chieftain after he abandoned Galveston in 1821. The Lafitte Papers record that—after spreading various rumors that he had been wounded and died at Caracas in May of 1821, had perished from sickness in Merida in 1825, and had also died and was buried in Silan in 1826—Lafitte continued with his privateering operations in the Gulf of Mexico and the Caribbean Sea. Never establishing any well-equipped bases as he did at Barataria and Galveston, but moving from place to place, his forays led him to the Yucatan peninsula, Isla Mujeres, Cartagena, Cuba, Isle

Articles of Piracy signed by Jean Laffite to Juan Juanvilles (Never before published—from the William D. Simpson Galveston Collection)

Instructions données Par Jn Laffite à Mr
Jn Juanvilles, Capitaine du Corsaire Français
nommé Le Confiant ... Galveston le 9 Mai 1817.
Il est permis au Capitaine de Capturer les
navires battant pavillon Britannique ou Espagnol
avec les marchandises dont il peut avoir besoin,
et il s'acquittera du montant de ses penses
par un certificat de paiement sur le Compte
de Mr. Andre Robin négociant de nouvelle Orleans.

Si le capitaine naviguait sur un bâtiment
Capturé, il devrait s'amcer à l'embouchure
de la Galveston avec un drapeau blanc sur
le mât de misaine et aucun autre.

Le capitaine de la commune Galveston répondra
à son signal en hissant un drapeau de la
même coleur en haut du clocher à l'entrée
du chenal.

Le Capitaine doit reconnaître chacun des
navires ancrés dans le chenal ou à l'intérieur
pour savoir s'ils m'ont à bord que le drapeau
de reconnaissance quand le navire Corsaire
est prêt à entrer il doit tirer un coup

de canon pour annoncer son arrivée et le fort tirera un coup de canon pour repondre de son signal.

Charte partie pour le Corsaire François nommé Le Confiant.

Aujourd'hui neuvième Mai mil huit cent dix Sept il est compris et arrêté entre nous, armateur, Capitaine, officiers, et Equipage du Corsaire François nommé Confiant de ce qui suit - Savoir:

Art 1er

La moitié de tout les cargaisons qui seront capturées appartiendra de droit à l'armateur.

Art 2e

Le Capitaine retirera une Commission de cinq pour cent sur le produit nets revenant à l'equipage.

Art 3e

Toutes les armes de guerre qui se trouveront à bord d'une prise reviendront de droit à l'armateur.

Art 7me.

Il ne sera permis à aucun homme en service pendant une Croisière de patronner tout établissement dans lequel on vend de l'alcool ou bien toute maison de prostitution ou de mauvaise Conduite.

Art 8.

Capitaine Jn Juanvilles doit se rappeler qu'il ne lui est permis sous aucun prétexte de mouiller dans un autre port qui celui de Galveston...

Toutes les parts de prises seront distribuées de la manière suivante. Savoir: au capitaine sept parts – 7.

Au Lieutenant quatre parts – 4.

Au maître d'Equipage trois – 3.

Au maître Canonier deux – 2.

Au Cuisinier deux parts – 2.

A chaque homme du reste de l'equipage – 2.

Tout ce que ci-dessus à été convenu et arrêté entre nous armateur, Capitaine, officiers et matelots, Promettons de nous y conformer en tout et de n'y rien changer, fait et de bonne foi à Galveston le 9 Mai 1817. Commandant:

J^n Laffite

Translation of *Articles of Piracy*
Jean Laffite to Juan Juanvilles*:

Instructions given by Jean Laffite to Mr. Juan Juanvilles, captain of the French corsair named The Confiant...Galveston the 9th of May 1817. The captain is permitted to capture the fighting ships flying the colors of England or Spain with whatever supplies he needs and he will pay his accumulated expenses with a certificate of payment on the account of Mr. Andre Robin, merchant of New Orleans.

If the captain is sailing a captured ship, he should identify himself at the opening of Galveston (Bay) with a white flag on the foremast and no other.

The captain of the Galveston settlement will reply to his signal by hoisting a flag of the same color atop the belfry at the entrance of the channel.

The captain should recognize each of the ships anchored in the channel or in the interior in order to tell if they are known to me as soon as the flag is recognized. When the corsair ship is ready to enter it should fire the cannon to announce its arrival and the port will fire the cannon in reply to its signal.

Freight contract for the French corsair named

Le Confiant

Today, May 9, 1817, it is understood and agreed among us, owner, captain, officers and crew of the French corsair named Confiant, on that which follows—Be it known:

1st Article

Half of all the captured cargo will belong by right to the owner.

2nd Article

The captain shall receive a commission of five percent of the net product accruing to the crew.

3rd Article

All the arms of war that are found on board a siezed ship shall belong by right to the owner.

(4-6 Articles missing)

7th Article

No man in service shall be permitted during a cruising to patronize either an establishment in which liquor is sold or a house of prostitution or of bad conduct.

8th Article

Captain Juan Juanvilles should remember that he is not permitted under any pretex whatsoever to drop anchor in any other port than that of Galveston...

All the parts of the prizes shall be distributed in the following manner:

To the Captain seven parts—7
To the Lieutenant four parts—4
To the Boatswain three—3
To the chief Cannoneer two—2
To the cook two parts—2
To each remaining man in the crew—2

All the above has been acknowledged and agreed upon among us, owner, Captain, officers and seamen, our ready promises conform to it in everything and to not changing any part of it. Made in good faith in Galveston May 9, 1817.

Commandant:
Jn Laffite

Translation by Pam Smith.

*Juan Juanvilles—also known as Juan Juanillio, Johanni, Giovanni, Gianni Barbafume, Jonny Barbe en Fume, Gianni Barbe en Feu, Johnny Beard-on-fire, Johnny Fire Whiskers, Johnny Red Beard; took part in the Battle of New Orleans as Sergeant Francois Sapia.

of Pines, St. Augustine, Santo Domingo, St. Kitts, Nevis, Guadeloupe, St. Croix, Martinique, Baltimore and Vera Cruz.

This family collection of papers further disclose that in 1832, at Charleston, South Carolina, Jean Lafitte married Emma Hortense Mortimore and moved to St. Louis, living under the assumed name of John Lafflin. There he played the role of a quiet citizen, using a gunpowder manufacturing business as a front while he cashed in on his captured loot, or as he put it, his "merchandise". From the year 1845 through 1850, Lafitte wrote his memoirs in a journal book, detailing the accounts of his life and sermonizing on the events of the time with which he was concerned. Recordation in the family Bible shows that he died at Alton, Illinois on May 5, 1854.

According to John A. Lafitte (a retired railroad engineer who died at Columbia, South Carolina in 1970) the Lafitte Papers were inherited by him in 1924 from the estate of his grandfather Jules Jean Lafitte, who was the son of the Galveston pirate captain Jean Lafitte. Included in the Papers was the journal book of memoirs—handwritten in French and signed and dated in many places by "Jn Laffite". John A. Lafitte later had these memoirs translated by two New Orleans nuns and published in 1958 by the Vantage Press as *The Journal of Jean Laffite—The Privateer-Patriot's Own Story.*

The original journal book of memoirs and the rest of the Lafitte Papers were sold to the rare document dealer William Simpson in 1969. Simpson sold the Papers, in 1976, to Governor Price Daniel who subsequently donated them to the Sam Houston Library and Research Center where they can now be seen.

Because the Lafitte Papers contain a wealth of historical information previously unknown or in dispute, it is important that their authenticity be established. Work has already been started in this direction by John Howells of Houston, an avid Lafitte researcher, who became summarily interested in the

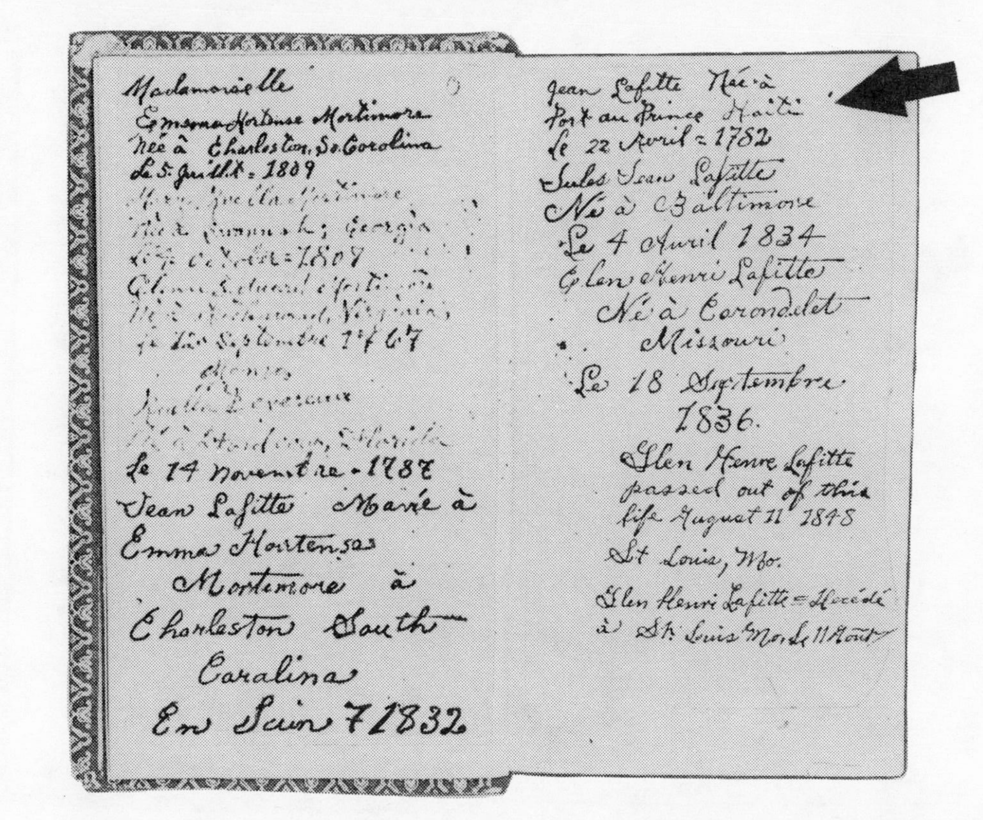

Madamoiselle
Emma Hortense Mortimore
Née à Charleston, So. Carolina
Le 5 Juillet = 1809

Le 14 novembre - 1787
Jean Lafitte Marié à
Emma Hortense
Mortimore à
Charleston South
Caralina
En Juin 7 1832

Jean Lafitte Née à
Port au Prince Haiti
Le 22 Avril = 1782
Jules Jean Lafitte
Né à Baltimore
Le 4 Avril 1834
Glen Henri Lafitte
Né à Corondelet
Missouri
Le 18 Septembre
1836.
Glen Henre Lafitte
passed out of this
life August 11 1848
St Louis, Mo.

Entry in Lafitte Family Bible showing place and birthdate of Jean Lafitte.

May 5th 1854 Alton Illinois
Our Father died Will be with
[illegible] brother Glenn Henri Will be
with Uncle Pierre in Heaven

Jean Lafitte Décédé le 5 Mai 1854
à Alton Illinois.

Mama
Emma Lafitte
Décédée le 17 Decembre
1885
Philadelphia

Jules Jean Lafitte; More:
Carmen Ernestine Andrechyne June 10 1863
Julius Jean Lafitte United in holy
Matrimony to Miss
Carmen Ernestina Andrechyne
June 10 1863
Leon Jean Né le 10 Mars 1865 Louisiane
Clemente Henri Né le 5 Février
1868 Louisiana
Clemente Henri Lafitte décédé
le 10 Juillet 1880 à St Louis Mo
Our little Son Clemente Henri
Parted from this life with fever
and passed on to the beyond
July 10 = 1880 St Louis, Mo.

Ernestina Lafitte
Décédée le Janvier 7 1912
Santa Clara, Cuba.

Lafitte family Bible entries showing place and date of death of Jean Lafitte.

famous privateer after he married Miss Jean Lafitte of New Orleans—a relative descendant of the like-named corsair.

Howells, because of his vocation as an Internal Revenue Service officer, was well qualified to undertake such an investigation. Concentrating primarily on the Lafitte journal of memoirs, he located—in the Federal Records Center at Fort Worth, Texas and in the Texas Archives at Austin, from the Mirabeau B. Lamar Papers—three original documents known to have been written and signed by Jean Laffite (Lafitte usually spelled his name with a "ff"; rarely with a "tt"—he was most commonly known, however, as "Lafitte") and had those documents compared to the Lafitte journal by Ralph O. Queen, an experienced professional handwriting expert. Queen confirmed that the documents were all written by the same man. The paper of the Lafitte journal was found to be made of linen base—a type used up to 1850—and the iron oxide ink used by the writer further vouched for its authenticity of age.

If the Lafitte Papers can be proved authentic, not only will they be useful as primary source material for historians, but they will be invaluable as clues for those who seek to find buried treasures. For instance, the journal reveals that one huge amount of gold was buried by his officers seven leagues west and two leagues north of San Augustine (which would place it somewhere on the right bank of St. John's River opposite Green Cove Springs, Florida). Laffite admitted that he did not know its exact location for his men were subsequently killed and their papers destroyed.

Lafitte also made mention in his journal that it was true of his having "hidden gold and silver on the sandy islands all along the Gulf Coast", and that he never wanted "to go back to Texas". If the pirate captain never returned to Texas, as he thus stated, it is one more reason why the many sandy islands around Galveston Bay may still hold some of his buried treasures.

During his investigation of the Lafitte Papers, John Howells noted that several pages of the original Lafitte journal were missing—having been obviously cut out of the section where Lafitte began revealing the locations of some of his hidden booty. Someone who had access to the journal in earlier days must have considered those particular pages very important; important enough to cut and remove them from out of the book. If those missing pages *do* contain information about the location of Lafitte's treasures, their recovery would not only reveal more prime historical material, but they would give their holder the best possible means to find some of the pirate chief's buried loot . . . original handwritten directions from Lafitte himself!

If the Lafitte journal is authentic, a fortune certainly awaits the finder of that document's missing pages. Another rare opportunity to cash in on paper profits.

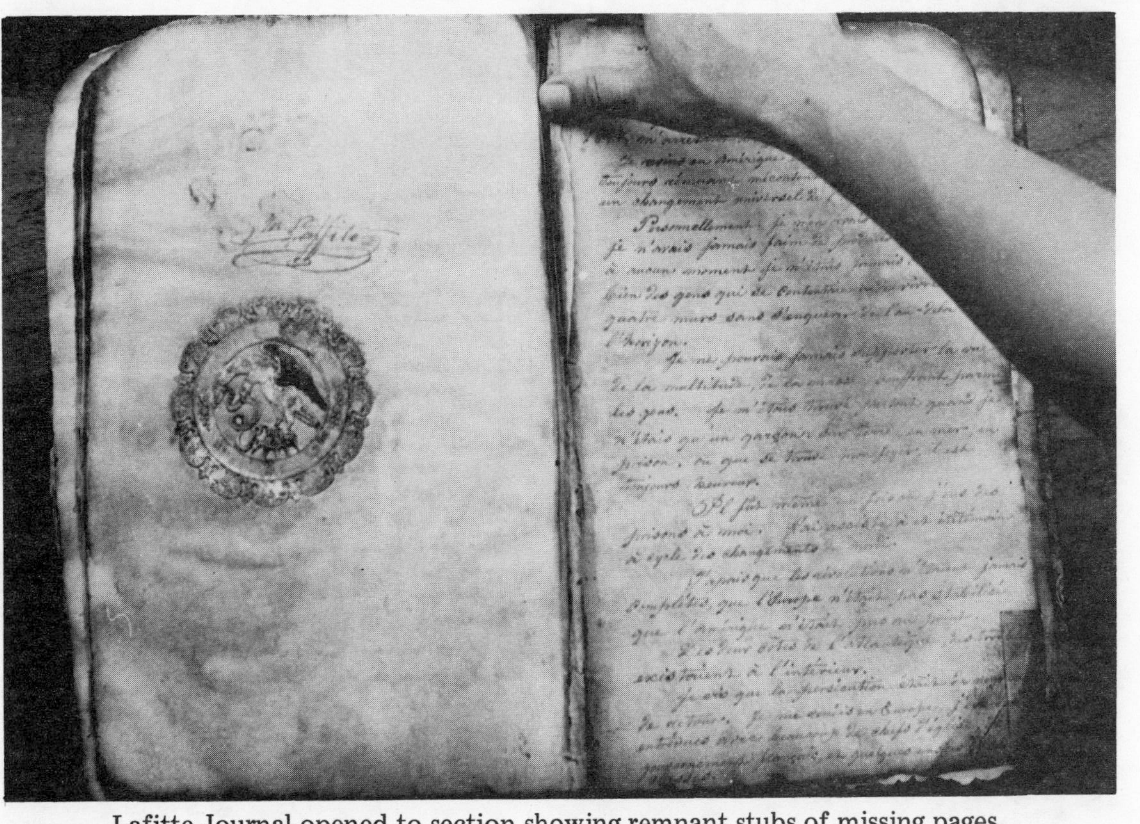

Lafitte Journal opened to section showing remnant stubs of missing pages.

[illegible] général De Arury [illegible]
dite Saint Louis. Le général L'allemand voyoit son
oeuvre coloniale couronnée de succès l'ambassadeur d'Es-
pagne à Washington, Luis De Onis éleva des protestations
enflammées contre les immigrants francois, affirmant que
le Texas étoit toujours province espagnole.

Sa méfiance, toujours en éveil à l'égard de nos
méthodes d'opposition ne faisant que grandir. Nos
méthodes donnaient d'excellents résultats: à Washington
et à la Nouvelle Orléans, quelques rares hommes d'affaires,
ne pouvant traiter nous, complotaient indirectement
contre nous, ils cétoient soumis à l'influence de l'ambassadeur à Washington, De Onis.

Jn Laffite

Page from the original journal book of memoirs—
"Laffite Journal"

Translation: by Pam Smith

...in the place of General De Arury on the island called Saint Louis (Galveston). General L'allemand saw his colonial work crowned with success. The Spanish ambassador to Washington, Luis De Onis, raised enflamed protests against the French immigrants, declaring that Texas was always a Spanish country.

His distrust, always on the guard with regard to our methods of opposition, can not help but grow. Our methods were giving excellent results: In Washington and in New Orleans, some exceptional businessmen, not being able to exploit us, plotted indirectly against us, they were amenable to the influence of the ambassador in Washington, De Onis.

Jn Laffite

Chapter Eleven

Skeleton Ships and Ghost Towns

The breezy air on Galveston beach was suddenly split with wild Indian warwhoops one morning, in the summer of 1820. Lafitte and his cohorts stumbled out of their tents and houses, priming weapons, drawing swords and knives in a hurried effort to ready themselves for an attack by the savages who lived half-way down the island. But the attack never came. Instead, the warwhoops got louder and strangely happier, but no closer. The pirates cautiously crept over the dunes that separated the village from the beach, and were confronted with a totally unexpected event.

There, on the beach—at the foot of what is now 18th Street—was the wildest scene that the buccaneers had ever witnessed: half-naked Indians, yelling and weaving around in the sand, waving in the air what appeared to be wine bottles; while, from the surf came more redmen carrying wooden crates filled with bottled liquid. From the crazed antics and vociferous conduct of the wildmen, the pirates soon fathomed that the Indians were not on the war-path, but were gloriously drunk. The intoxicating liquor was being salvaged from the wine cargo of a French schooner that had been wrecked out in the surf, and the native Americans were having what was probably the first Galveston beach party.

The schooner eventually broke up and the remainder of its cargo sank to the bottom of the sea. Although one hundred and fifty years of aging would certainly not improve the wine, it *would* improve the value of the bottles and the rest of the cargo that was on board. Bottle collectors and antique dealers will pay considerable sums for such relics; so bathers, playing in the sand, on the beach at the foot of 18th Street should keep a sharp look-out for that treasure hoard of ancient bottles and French antiques.

After Lafitte abandoned his pirate village of Campeche, the shores of Galveston Bay began to see the arrival of colonists bound to make their fortune at the new frontier in Texas. Every ship that brought them was loaded with essential supplies and the life-savings of the settlers. Because of storms or the ship captains' unfamiliarity with the treacherous bar that guarded the pass to Galveston Bay, many of these heavily provisioned vessels were wrecked and sunk; their valuable cargos surrendered to the bottom of the sea where they still remain . . . a fortune to be found by modern-day Texas adventurers.

The schooner *Call* was one such ship. On April 5, 1831, she was wrecked off Boliver Point just across the harbor from Lafitte's deserted fortress. A few days later, the schooner *Climax* suffered the same fate. The brig *Gerhardt Herman*—transporting German emigrants to Texas—was wrecked at the west end of Galveston Island on December 31, 1846; the emigrants were all saved, but their valuables were lost to the sea along with the ship. In the middle of Galveston Bay, Redfish Reef also claimed the cargos of the *Rising Sun* and the 100-ton schooner *Mary*.

The treacherous bar that once existed at the entrance to Galveston's harbor, claimed the prize cargoes, supplies and armaments of the Texas Navy ships *Brutus* and *Invincible*, that went aground and sank there after an engagement with the Mexican Navy in the summer of 1837.

After the Texans gained independence from Santa Anna's dictator government, the threat of invasion from Mexico still loomed and the young republic of Texas needed aid to thwart that danger. Help came from an unexpected source . . . Cuba. Sympathizing with the Texas cause, the ladies of Havana donated their gold jewelry to be melted down and sold, so that two brass cannons could be made and sent to the Texians. These two cannons found their use aboard the privateer *Tom Toby* and helped plague the Mexican Navy during that perilous time.

On the sixth of October, in 1837, a bad storm caught the *Tom Toby* and 20 to 25 other vessels in the Galveston harbor, driving them across the bay to be wrecked at Virginia Point. The two brass cannons on the *Tom Toby* were recovered later in 1879, but all of the other armament and cargos of those many other ships remain as sunken treasure . . . yet to be recovered.

During the Civil War, the Union gunboat *Clifton* was captured by Dick Dowling's Confederates at the Battle of Sabine Pass and pressed into service for the South. It later burned and sank, close to shore, about 100 yards off the present Sabine Pass west jetty. A build-up of sand has gradually covered the derelict creating an unusual shipwreck whose valuable cargo of Civil War relics could be recovered without the use of diving equipment.

Dry land hunting for relics of antiquity is certainly easier and more economically productive than underwater exploration. For that reason, some of the most prolific cornucopias for such treasures are the ghost towns, or abandoned villages, of the early Texans. The area around Galveston Bay abounds with these, since as most colonists arrived by boat, they usually settled close to the coast. Many of these settlements suffered hard times and soon vanished.

There are more than two hundred ghost towns within fifty leagues of the bay; some of the most impressive ones border on the bay itself. South Galveston, for instance, located about half-way down the island at Lake Como, once boasted a population of 3,000 people, fine homes, a hotel and a race track. Started in 1895, this large resort was wiped out by the great hurricane of 1900. Those who enjoy finding old coins would do well to search the site of its race track, for coins have a habit of falling out from the pockets of men sitting in grandstands, and race-horse fans have been known to carry fair sums of money to the track.

One mile east of South Galveston, is the ghost town of Nottingham. Built in 1892, around a lace factory that employed over two hundred Irish girls, the village, its railroad depot, stores and saloons were also destroyed by the 1900 hurricane. Today, only the brick foundations and two large dyeing vats of the lace factory mark the site, however, from an aerial view one can still see the outlines of the multitude of streets that once formed the west Galveston town of Nottingham.

Relic hunters need to travel only a few miles from Nottingham to find another one of the principle ghost towns of Galveston Bay . . . San Luis. Built in 1838 on the island of San Luis, just west of Galveston Island, the town of San Luis grew to a population of 2,000 by 1843. Attracting considerable commerce with its 1,000 foot wharf, this enterprizing sea port established two newspapers, several hotels, general stores, warehouses and a 2½-story inn—nestled among 20-foot tall oleanders—that furnished entertainment and refreshment for the early Texas seafarers and settlers.

The first cotton compress and the first steamboat in Texas were built at San Luis. Such ingenuity, however, was countered by the erroneous plan of having located the town on such a low-lying island as San Luis. High tides and storm waters continuously inundated the thriving village and by 1844, everyone had moved away and the town was abandoned. A 30-foot wide brick cistern remains as a hidden monument to this once potentially great seaport of the Gulf Coast.

Along the shores of Galveston Bay, there are many other smaller ghost towns which offer excellent opportunities for finding lost relics.

North Galveston, located at Eagle Point, was built in 1840 and had a post office, church and stage line until it was wiped out by the 1915 hurricane. The same fate happened to the village of Virginia at Virginia Point. Early maps show the existence of Powhattan at Moses Lake between 1837 and 1854, and near Eagle Point and along the shoreline between San Leon and Kemah, the towns of Austinia, Rock Spring and Flander's Grove were charted between 1839 and 1856. None of these towns are in existence today.

At Red Bluff, a settlement of the same name existed between 1880 and 1890, having a general store, church, school and post office. On Bolivar Point, Fort Casas was the name given by Gen. James Long to his settlement of 200 men in 1820. Later, in 1876, the town of Ishmael was platted at the same end of the Bolivar Peninsula, but today, there is no visible evidence of either Fort Casas or Ishmael.

Many valuable coins have been found along the north shoreline at Morgan's Point, which is the site of the ghost town of New Washington. The warehouses and wharves of this embryonic port were destroyed by General Santa Anna's troops just before the battle at San Jacinto, and the town never rebuilt.

Several miles from Clear Lake, where Bay Area Boulevard now crosses Armand Bayou, the Old French Settlement, or town of Middle Bayou, was founded in 1824 by several French families who grew vegetables and used the waterways of the bayou, lakes and bays to transport their produce to market by barge-boats. At one time, this community had a post office and a school. David Harris, the founder of Harrisburg, died at his son's home at Middle Bayou in 1841; since then the settlement gradually vanished and now only a few grave markers on the north side of Big Island Slough remain as evidence of this pioneer group.

In 1822, Nathaniel Lynch started the town of Lynchburg on the north side of Buffalo Bayou at its confluence with the San Jacinto River. Here, he operated a ferry and erected a steammill, tavern and small general store. When a group of early

Texas revolutionists stopped by Lynch's in 1835, his wife Frances sewed them a battle flag—the first lone star banner of Texas.

Taking four yards of blue silk, donated by Captain William Scott, she sewed a piece of domestic to protect its edge and with the help of Charles Zanco (who later died in the Alamo) painted a large 5-pointed star in the center with the word "Independence" under it. Thus was created the first lone star banner of Texas. Coincidently, it also created the first armed clash between Texian colonists.

At the settlement of Harrisburg, another volunteer company of militia heard of the flag and its motto and announced that they would shoot anyone raising an unofficial flag. The thirty members of the Lynchburg Company lost no time in inviting the Harrisburgers to come and see their flag hoisted. The following day at noon, two yawls carrying sixteen armed men from Harrisburg sailed up to the shore in front of Mrs. Lynch's house; standing in a line between the shore and the house, Captain Scott and his men stood—armed and waiting.

James S. McGahey set his gun against the house, went inside and brought out Mrs. Lynch's flag which he proceeded to unfurl and then planted its staff into the bank of the San Jacinto River . . . its lone star waving flauntingly in the breeze. After a few seconds, the men from Harrisburg pushed their boats back into the river, took off their hats which they waved and then shouted "Hurrah for the lone star!" These same men later took this flag with them to defeat the Mexican Army in the Battle of Concepción at San Antonio, on October 28, 1835. The town of Lynchburg thus reserved the distinction of having contributed the first lone star emblem to be identified with Texas. By 1840, Lynchburg grew to a population of 205, but today, only a ferryboat landing and a few homes mark the site of the once busy ferry town and birthplace of the lone star of Texas.

Across Buffalo Bayou, Lynch also laid out the town of San Jacinto in 1836, and by 1840 it also became a sizeable community. Today, however, there is nothing at San Jacinto but the Lynchburg Crossing restaurant. Because of subsidence, water creeping over the ghost town of San Jacinto will soon make its relics and historical objects harder to find and further bury the memory of that village of early Texans.

Treasure hunters will have to work fast to stay on dry land in this rapidly sinking area or the valuable artifacts of the past will soon be lost forever.

Chapter Twelve

Money Holes

Eight Million Dollars in gold is buried six leagues north of Galveston Bay on the banks of Bowie Creek. Shortly before his death, J. Frank Dobie wrote of two East Texas men, J. R. Jamison and Sambo Reeves, who professed to know the exact location of this money hole.

Thirty six hundred pounds of gold—12 jack-loads of 36 gold bars, each weighing 100 pounds—was buried in the eighteenth century by a Spanish military escort after an Indian attack at Bowie Creek, near the present town of Dayton. The few surviving Spaniards did not want part of any future Indian attacks, so before they left the scene of the battle they buried the gold along with their dead comrades, Indians and animals. There is no record of the Spanish ever returning to recover the hidden cache.

In 1900, a Mexican with a way-bill appeared at the site, looked for certain markings on trees, dug a few holes and, after several weeks departed empty-handed. This seemed to revive a bit of gold fever around Bowie Creek.

A family of Negroes that lived nearby began hearing voices of the spirits of the Spanish soldiers and saw lights coming out of the ground and dancing on the surface to point the way to the money hole. After digging at the revealed location, about 10 feet down, they struck a copper chest; making a hole in the top, they could see the gold bars stacked inside. Greatly excited, they tried to lift the chest out, but it was too heavy. They pulled up two large fence posts and attempted to wedge the chest out of the hole, but only succeeded in easing it into a strata of quicksand that their digging had uncovered; the chest sank out of sight.

Sambo Reeves was determined to get that gold. A bull dozer was hired to dig into the money hole, however, the quicksand soon cut short its use; then a drag-line was brought in, but the quicksand filled the hole as fast as its bucket could dig. Finally, suction pumps were used, but in the middle of the operation, in 1957, a Trinity River flood backed water up Bowie Creek and into the money hole, and the work was suspended. Since then, no one has seen fit to spend any more time or money in recovering this $8,000,000 hoard of gold.

A smaller money hole was discovered in the late 1880's when the young daughter of Albert Rasch's widow found a can full of gold coins worth $5,000 while playing under her house in Houston. The late Rasch, it seems, did not believe in banks, and had evidently stashed his money around in various places without informing his family of all of the locations. A search in the deed records of Harris County ought to reveal the location of Albert Rasch's home, and it is possible that there might be a few more cans full of gold buried around that site.

Some of Lafitte's pirates hid their small fortunes in money holes around Virginia Point and Eagle Grove, if one can believe the tales told by them to Charles Hooten, when he visited Galveston Island in 1841. Lafitte's first mate actually sang him a song about buried treasure and reveled in bragging about the money that he had hidden away from his house.

One of the last three Lafitte seamen left on Galveston Island told, on his death bed, of burying many treasures, marking trees, taking compass bearings and not being able to refind his loot at a later time. One of these caches was evidently found in 1857, when some doubloons and Indian relics were dug up about two miles south of the Texas City docks near the site of pirate Jim Campbell's house.

Dr. Reginald Wilson, of Dayton, Texas, recalls one of his patients telling him of finding an old pistol among some fortress ruins about 200 yards back from the shore of Tabbs Bay at Evergreen Point, not far from Sam Houston's 1842-1863 homesite at Cedar Point. Old timers in the area believe the ruins to have been built and used by Lafitte. This location coincides with the directions to a fort that Lafitte described in his journal as being 21 kilometers from the Trinity River and 45 kilometers from Galveston. After the 1818 storm, Lafitte sent four carpenters, five masons, and two blacksmiths to repair the fortifications. Certainly the area around this bay fortress should not be overlooked as a possible burial place for some of the many treasures that Lafitte left along the Gulf, as he admitted in his journal.

Being a Frenchman, Lafitte seemed to favor Gallic men in his organization. LaPorte was his bookkeeper, Rousselin his collector, and Arsene Lacarriere Latour was his confidant and adviser. Latour often used the assumed name of *John Williams* in his dealings with Lafitte and officials in New Orleans and Cuba. After Lafitte abandoned Galveston, Latour, or Williams, went to Cuba and helped build roads at Havana until 1823; then he suddenly disappeared and was not heard from again until his death in France in 1837.

In 1824, a John Williams applied for and received from Stephen Austin a grant of a league and a labor of land on Clear Creek where the Gulf Freeway now crosses that stream. In April of 1825, Williams offered to sell his land and improvements to his neighbor John Dickinson. The price was $100 cash and 12 gentle Spanish horses. Dickinson was killed by Indians at San Antonio before the deal was consummated, so the land was ultimately sold to William Vince; John Williams then faded out of history.

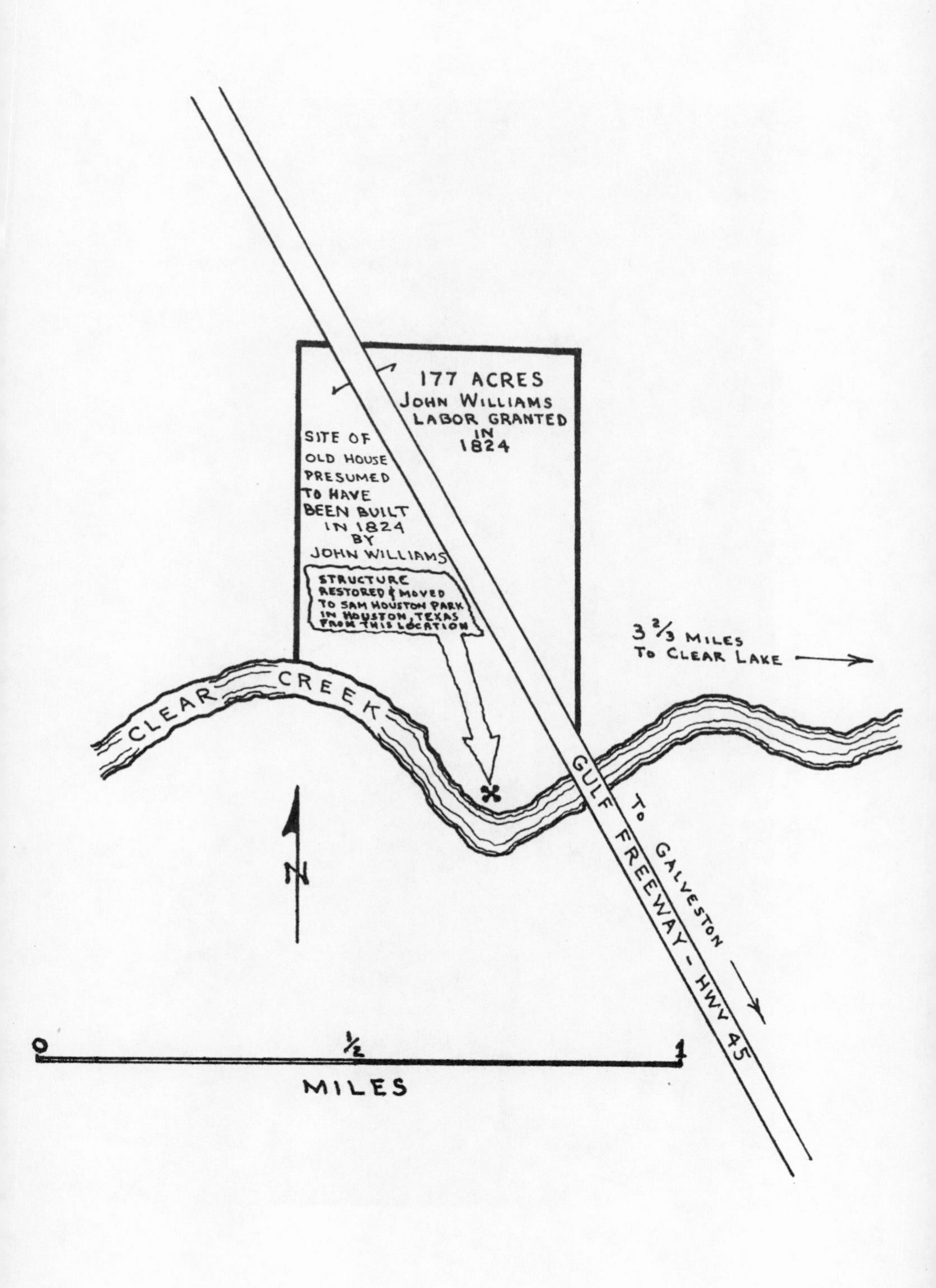
177 ACRES
JOHN WILLIAMS
LABOR GRANTED
IN
1824
SITE OF
OLD HOUSE
PRESUMED
TO HAVE
BEEN BUILT
IN 1824
BY
JOHN WILLIAMS
STRUCTURE
RESTORED & MOVED
TO SAM HOUSTON PARK
IN HOUSTON, TEXAS
FROM THIS LOCATION
3 2/3 MILES
TO CLEAR LAKE
CLEAR CREEK
N
GULF FREEWAY - HWY 45
TO GALVESTON
0
1/2
1
MILES

Clear Creek site of John William's home.

Restored home of John Williams.

Where did he go? What did he want *12* horses for if he was divesting himself of land to keep them on? Could the John Williams of Clear Creek be the same John Williams *alias* Arsene Latour—Lafitte's henchman? Could he have needed 12 gentle horses to carry away a pirate hoard which he kept at his place on the creek? If so, was he successful in finding 12 other horses—not Dickinson's—or could he have left *some* of his treasure still buried somewhere along Clear Creek near the Gulf Freeway?

The number "12" often seems to crop up when it comes to transporting gold. Regard the 12 jack loads at Bowie Creek. Turn the number 12 around and you nave 21—Black Jack!

Lafitte was a swarthy Frenchman; some said that at times his countenance was even *black*. His first name Jean is the same as John or *Jack*. Black Jack again.

Near Smith's Point is a bird sanctuary for the Roseate Spoonbill, called Vingt Un Island. Vingt Un are French words meaning the number "21"—*Violá!* Black Jack again. Vingt Un—a French Black Jack—might be a clue as to the name of Jean Lafitte's special treasure island, and a numerologist might make something out of the fact that Lafitte admitted, in his journal, that it was true he had hidden gold and silver on the sandy islands along the Gulf Coast when he left Galveston Island in the year 18*21!*

Captain "Robbie" Strasding, a retired ship captain from Kemah, testifies that some of the descendants of Lafitte's followers who moved to the Kemah area, when the Galveston pirate camp was abandoned, told him that Lafitte's treasure was buried on Vingt Un Island. Many years ago, Captain Strasding searched the island but only found a few Indian arrowheads, however, he did not have the aid of modern-day metal detection equipment—he only looked on the surface of the shell-covered cay.

GALVESTON BAY

Day sailors who are fortunate enough to cast eyes upon one of the Roseate Spoonbills flying across Galveston Bay, might do well to follow that beautiful bird and perhaps become a real winner at Vingt Un . . . 21 . . . Black Jack!

Chapter Thirteen

The Old Man and His Gold Machine

Anyone can hunt for buried treasure. The only tool really needed is a shovel. Shoveling, however, requires a lot of physical effort, and it is not long before an anxious treasure hunter gets tired and discouraged. There are a few other aids that will greatly ease the labor of treasure explorations. One of these is the use of a probe—a slender rod that can be shoved deep into the ground. This will quickly indicate the presence of any large buried object, but, of course, the probe might slide through any scattered coins or small objects; so it is of use only when looking for bulky prizes. A metal rod with one end sharpened and a "T" handle welded on the other end makes an excellent probe. It should not be much longer than eight or nine feet so that it can be easily transported and stored.

A great deal of exploratory digging and probing can be done away with by the use of a metal detector. This instrument is carried by the person, and usually has a handle with an electronic signal loop affixed to its end. A battery power supply creates an electric field around this loop, and when any metal object crosses this field it disturbs the circuit; this is indicated by a visual meter or an audible sound that informs the operator of the metal's proximity. By holding the loop close to the ground, and passing it over the area to be explored, the presence of any buried metal objects is easily detected. Quite a large area can be covered in a short time by the use of such an instrument.

Metal-detecting around old cystern at site of Lafitte's fortress at Galveston in 1965.

There is a considerable number of good, light, transistorized metal detectors on the market today at very reasonable prices. Some of these weigh less than two pounds and can be carried all day without tiring the operator. These detectors are sensitive enough to locate the smallest of coins that might be buried just under the surface of the ground, or larger metal objects buried much deeper in the earth.

Many interesting objects other than gold or silver can be found with these devices. Dr. A. H. Grove found a small cannon ball near the site of Jean Lafitte's "Maison Rouge" while searching with his metal detector in the summer of 1965.

The use of modern diving gear such as the SCUBA (self contained underwater breathing apparatus) also opens new horizons to the treasure hunter. Today, he can explore with ease many heretofore unsearched areas and sunken ships that, in the past, were inaccessible because of the old-fashioned diving suits and their unwieldy attached air hoses. The new compact SCUBA gear is completely portable and the whole unit is attached and carried on the body of the diver. This makes an ideal thing for exploring the many sunken treasure wrecks that have not had their fortunes tapped.

There are some people who claim to have divining rod instruments that will seek out gold and silver much like the old "water dowsers" used to locate underground water reservoirs. Whenever a rancher wanted to dig a water well, he would hire one of these old-timers to locate the water. The "dowser" would cut a forked branch from a witch hazel, peach or willow tree, and grasping the two forks in his hands, would walk around with this wand extended in front of him, until he felt this divining rod tug and point to the ground. It was at this spot that he would direct the digging to be . . . and it was at this spot that the water was usually found. The accuracy of these water witchers was uncanny. Not everyone could get the "feel" of

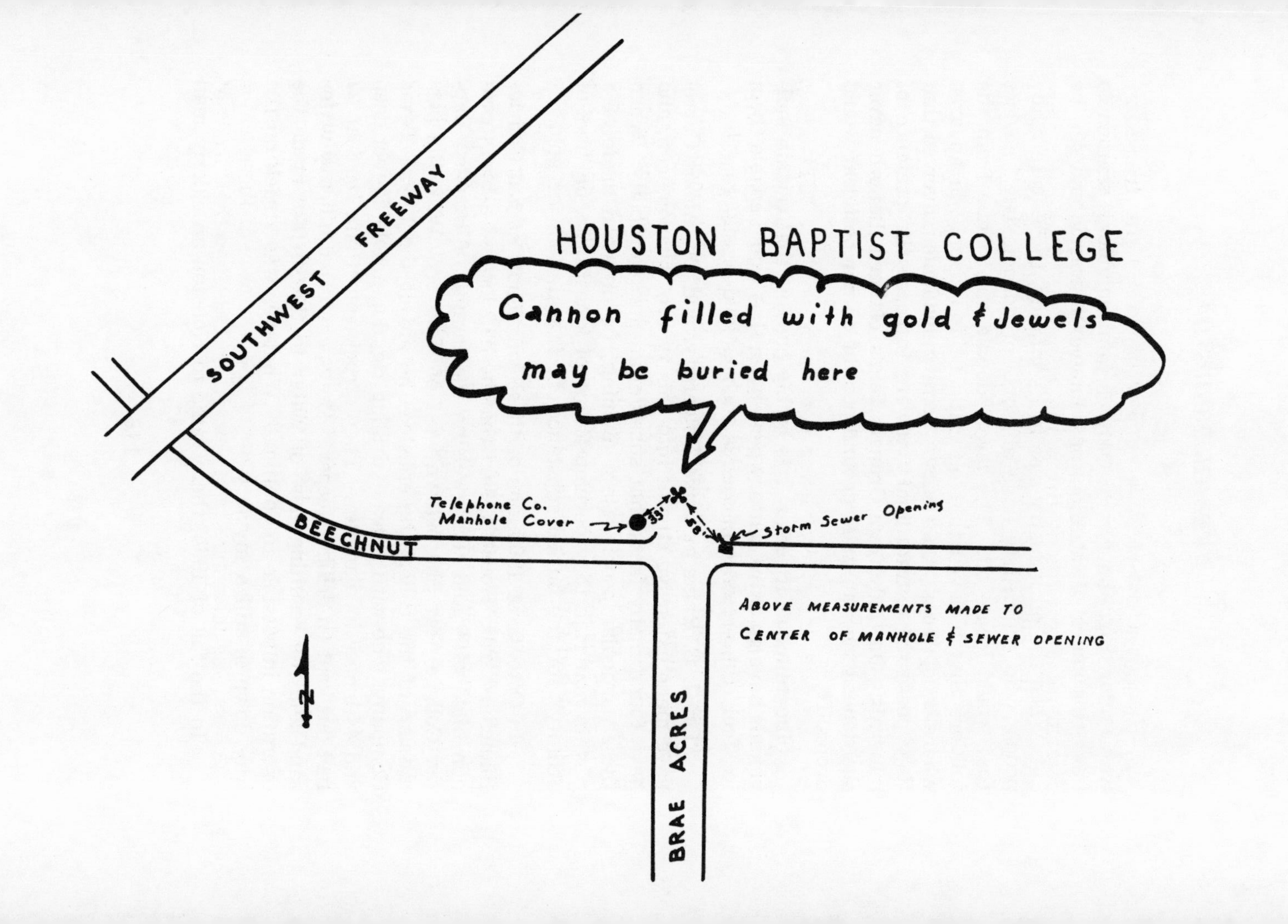
HOUSTON BAPTIST COLLEGE
Cannon filled with gold & Jewels may be buried here
SOUTHWEST FREEWAY
BEECHNUT
Telephone Co. Manhole Cover
39'
58'
Storm Sewer Opening
BRAE ACRES
ABOVE MEASUREMENTS MADE TO CENTER OF MANHOLE & SEWER OPENING
N

water "dowsing," however. Only certain individuals seemed to have this knack of intuition, or whatever it was.

When the oil industry was in its infancy, there were many people who claimed to have all sorts of "doodle bug" devices that would locate oil. The term "doodle bug" came from the folklore that believed that oil could be found only in an area where doodle bugs would bury. Some individuals perceived that they possessed extraordinary powers to sense the presence of minerals. One lady from Orange, Texas, claimed that whenever she danced over an underground pool of oil her petticoat would drop off!

Incredible as it seems, it is highly possible that certain individuals have an extra sensory perception that would enable them to "feel" the presence of metals such as gold or silver.

Dr. J. B. Rhine at Duke University, and Dr. Alexis Carrel have made extensive studies into this type of phenomenon, and have found many facts that substantiate its plausibility. When these particular people use a divining rod or wand made of a certain material, they develop a sort of kinesthesia, or "feel of affinity" for the buried substance, be it water, oil or gold.

In October of 1965, one of these individuals named Charles Blanchard from Houston, said that he had located a brass cannon filled with gold and jewels on the campus of Houston Baptist College near Sharpstown west of Houston. With the permission of the college he enlisted the aid of the Layne Texas Company, who with a heavy drilling rig, dug a hole 40-feet deep and 44-inches in diameter. They struck something hard at 27 feet but kept on drilling deeper. They penetrated a heavy water sand and the resulting flow of water to the surface made the operation impossible to continue. Whatever was struck on the way down is still a mystery.

In the fall of 1964, there came to Houston an elderly man

from Florida, who had a gold finding instrument with which he said he found a Spanish treasure galleon that was sunk off the Florida coast near Fort Pierce. Over $2,000,000 in gold and silver coins were retrieved from this wreck of the 1715 Plate Fleet that went down along the coast during a hurricane. The story of this fantastic treasure find can be found in the many news accounts of that time.

This old gentleman had read in the newspapers of a group of prospectors digging for a treasure in a hillside near Belton, Texas. He had driven all the way from Florida to that digging site and used his instrument to see if the treasure really was there.

His instrument showed that there was no gold or silver whatsoever near the site where the group was digging. The newspapers later proved him right, for the expedition found nothing there. The old man, however, did get a reading of a large amount of gold near the lake at Belton, not 50 feet from the highway, at the base of a big oak tree.

The old-timer came to Houston then, to enlist the aid of some friend to bring trucks and help him get the gold and transport it back to Florida. While he was in Houston, with his fabulous gold-finding gadget, his friend prevailed upon him to check out some of the legendary treasure locations around the area.

Lafitte's Grove was his first stop.

Out near the windswept grove of Galveston Island, a passerby would have thought that the ghost of Jean Lafitte had returned—for such was the spectre of this quaint old character and his gold machine.

His very outside appearance conjured up the vision of what an island pirate might look like. He was a tall, agile man; over 70 years of age, and he wore a black beret cocked jauntily on one side of his head. Long sideburns grew down his ruddy cheeks, and a most villainous looking mustache, with twisted waxed ends, exploded out above his firm granite-like jaw. One side of his nose had been eaten off by radiation burns that he received while experimenting with adapting his machine to find uranium.

And that machine!

It was not so much a machine as it was a most ridiculous looking divining rod of sorts. To the small end of an ordinary fiberglass fishing rod, he had attached a threaded brass tip; there was a copper wire that ran from this tip, down along the rod to its butt end. He had several different weirdly shaped plexiglass cylindrical heads that he could screw onto the brass tip. These heads were about six inches in length and were filled with a secret formula which only he knew. He said that his gold-seeking head, among other ingredients, had $750 worth of gold in it. His silver-seeking head had a good quantity of silver involved in its making; he also had heads that were made out of copper, iron, and uranium. With each different head attached to the rod, he could seek out that particular element.

In the road in front of Lafitte's Grove, the old man affixed the gold-seeking head to the fiberglass rod. He put the butt of the rod into his stomach, with the end containing the gold-head sticking straight up into the air, and placed his feet firmly apart as if readying himself for some great ordeal. He squinted his eyes very intently at the head, and placed his fingers so that they made contact with the copper wire on the rod butt; then he slowly turned his body in a smooth searching sweep—suddenly, the gold-head bent toward the ground and seemed to be magnetized toward one spot! The old man's eyes lit up with a feverish gleam—

"There!" he exclaimed. "See there—? See where it's pointing? Lots of gold! . . . Let's see if there's any silver."

He quickly unscrewed the gold-head, and put on the silver one. The same routine was carried out and as his body turned in a line with the spot where the gold was indicated, the rod's head again bent down toward the same location—as if an invisible wire was pulling it down.

"Boy!" he yelled, "there is both gold and silver right there—just inside that fence!"

He rotated his body slightly and suddenly the rod dipped again! Another spot was pointed out! This one was still across the fence and on one side of the gate to the property on which the grove was located. Two treasure locations! . . . at Lafitte's Grove! The old man was really anxious to get to the treasure, but neither he nor his partner were able to get permission to enter the property and dig.

Thus daunted, they went out to the end of Galveston Island to San Luis Pass where he spotted over 20 shipwrecks with gold and silver in them out in the Gulf just off shore. None of these wrecks showed as much gold as the ship his machine found off the Florida coast, but his readings indicated that all of them had good quantities of the precious metal aboard.

The old man then went back to Houston, where he procured the yacht *Partly Cloudy* in which he could cruise up Buffalo Bayou in search of Santa Anna's gold buried along its banks. As the boat went up the bayou, he got no indication on his instrument until it reached the outlet of Sim's Bayou. There, where Samuel Allen once lived, his instrument pointed out three separate caches of gold! These were buried at the bases of three trees on the high south bank of Buffalo Bayou. There was no way to get off the boat or land at that part of the bayou, so the craft returned to port.

The old prospector then drove to the site of the old Beazley house at La Porte. He could find no reading or indication of any gold or silver whatsoever at that location—but his rod kept bending very strongly in the direction toward Red Bluff and the Kemah-Seabrook area. He then drove down the highway between La Porte and Seabrook; stopping to take a reading every two or three miles. There was nothing indicated at Red Bluff, but the pull from Seabrook was getting stronger, the closer he got!

As he approached Seabrook, his instrument showed gold and silver pulling from three different locations—one spot was pinpointed south-southeast of the mouth of Taylor Lake about 20 yards offshore out in the water of Clear Lake. No boat or dredging equipment was readily available, so the other two locations were then tracked down.

His gadget led him close to a small gulley that ran into Galveston Bay along the shoreline at Kemah. The owner of the property was contacted, but he had just finished building a fine home there, and did not want to allow anyone to dig in his yard. Needless to say, the old-timer did not give the landowner the exact location of the treasure, but led him to believe that it was in another spot. So the Kemah landowner might have a treasure of gold on his property—but he does not know where it is!

The remaining treasure pulled the old man's rod toward the north and led him to a fenced-in yard on the shore of Clear Creek. His instrument bent almost double as it pointed out two different spots within the yard.

"Looky there!" he shouted, "There's plenty of gold and silver buried in that there yard! Most I've ever seen in one place! See there!"

He could hardly pull the rod away from the fixation it had on the buried treasure. He would twist and pull his body about in fearful contortions, but the gold-head on the end of the rod seemed to be glued in the direction of the loot which he was certain to be buried in the yard.

As he did not have permission to enter the property, the old man had to wait four days before he could contact the owner and get permission to dig for the treasure. With permission being granted, the old man enlisted the aid of some friends to help him dig and carry the heavy gold and silver. They arrived at Seabrook and entered the yard. As the old man began to use his instrument, it took him to a spot not ten feet away from the water's edge. With his rod nearly bending double from the force of the pull, he determined that beneath that spot there was a large amount of gold and silver. The exotic metals were evidently in a huge iron chest, because he also got a strong indication when he put on his iron-seeking head.

The other treasure spot was located directly under a small sailboat that was dry-docked in the same yard. The old man grew greatly excited and exclaimed "There is more gold and silver at this point than at the other one! Let's dig!"

Immediately, the sailboat was moved aside and the shovels began to dig. A few pieces of broken glass were dug up first, then a piece of a leg off of a china doll, then a large piece of rusted iron was uncovered. About four feet down, a water sand level was reached, and the faster the men dug, the faster the hole would fill up with water—it was impossible to dig it out.

The old man looked discouragingly at the hole, and then reluctantly moved the diggers to the other spot, explaining that a heavy chest full of gold and silver might sink 15 to 20 feet deep in such a quick-like water sand. It would be useless to attempt to retrieve it by further digging.

Instead of digging at the remaining location, the old man figured that if the heavy chest had sunk as far as the water sand it would probably be as impossible to get as the other one; so the only hope would be that the chest lay between the surface of the ground and the grasping water sand. He plunged a ten-foot steel rod into the ground where his instrument indicated the gold to be; at four feet he again struck the water sand and the entire rod went down its full ten feet without hitting anything. It was useless to dig! There was plenty of gold and silver there all right, but it had sunk deep into the slushy water sand. The old man's eyes were almost tearful and his disappointment was quite evident—as he slowly and reluctantly packed his marvelous gold-finding machine in the car and left.

It was at this exact spot, some four months later, that the youth who was testing a metal detector, found some loose gold and silver Spanish coins dated from 1790 to 1806 buried under the ground with a human jawbone!

It was in the creek, directly in front of this spot, that Wesley Müecke pulled a human skull up in his seining nets, and on the shoreline in front of this spot, lay several old house foundation piers made out of hand-made bricks . . . piers from the old Keller home.

Did not the Kemah lady, who was a descendant of Jean Lafitte, believe that somewhere near the old Keller home, the pirate's treasure was buried?

The treasure may be there—but if so, it has sunk too far down in the sand for recovery, just as the old man said.

There are surely many more treasures buried around Galveston Bay, but they have either been forgotten about, or their locations have been kept a dark secret throughout the years.

Most of the treasure locations described in this book are factual; some are legendary and some are based upon suppositions. All have been mentioned, even the most dubious ones, in order to give as much information as possible to anyone who would like to begin the fascinating business of treasure hunting. There are enough buried treasures around Galveston Bay to keep a person looking forever!

GALVESTON BAY

Walk along the shorelines where the pirates once trod,
Drop your anchor in the waters where sunken galleons lay.
Search around the routes of the mighty marching armies.
Explore the old homesites where the early pioneers lived.
Look in your own back yard, for—

"Treasure is where you find it!"

Sources

Isla Serpiente, Map No. G-133 (1816) Rosenberg Library
Port of Galveston, Map No. G-4-27 (1828) Rosenberg Library
Map of Texas—1830, Pressler
Map of Texas—1830, Stephen F. Austin
Map of Texas—1844, W. H. Emory
Plan of The City of Galveston—1845, William H. Sandusky
Map of Proposed Site of Seabrook—c. 1894, Thomas Owen
Map of Texas—1856, J. H. Young
Le Champ d'Asile, L'Heritier
Le Champ d'Asile au Texas, C. . .D. . .
Early Times In Texas, J. C. Duval
A French Captain in Texas, Just Girard
Treasure Trove, Pirate's Gold, Gordon Cooper
El Codigo de los Piratas, Garcia Montero
Brethren of the Coast, P. C. Kemp; C. Lloyd
Doubloons, Charles B. Driscoll
Cabeza de Vaca's Adventures in the Unknown Interior of America (translation by Cyclone Covey)
Wave of the Gulf, Jesse A. Ziegler
Home On the Double Bayou, Ralph Jackson
Coronado's Children, J. Frank Dobie

True Stories of Old Houston and Houstonians, S. O. Young

History of North Mexican States and Texas, H. Bancroft

History of Texas, Henderson Yoakum

1,001 Lost, Buried or Sunken Treasures, Ferris Coffman

Secrets of Padre Island, Vernon Smylie

The History of South America and Mexico, John M. Niles

History of Galveston, O. Springer

The Mystery of San Jacinto, Andrew Forest Muir—*Southwest Review*

History of Fort Bend County, Wharton

Early History of Galveston, J. O. Dyer

United States Magazine and Democratic Review—July, 1839

Jean LaFitte—Gentlemen Rover, Stanley Arthur

Battle of Galveston, Robert M. Franklin

The Mexican Side of the Texas Revolution, C. E. Casteneda

The National Intelligencer, December 23, 1817

The Memoirs of a Buccaneer, Louis Le Golif

J. C. Clopper's Journal and Book of Memoranda for 1828, Quarterly of the Texas State Historical Association, XIII

Texas in 1837, Andrew F. Muir, ed.

A Visit to Texas, Author unknown

William Bollaert's Texas, William Bollaert

Texas and the Texans, Henry S. Foote

From Texas to California in 1849: Diary of C. C. Cox, Southwestern Historical Quarterly, XXIX

Narrative of Robert Hancock Hunter, 1813-1902, Robert Hancock Hunter

Reminiscences of Fifty Years in Texas, John J. Linn

The Evolution of a State; or, Recollections of Old Texas Days, Noah Smithwick

Guide to Texas Emigrants, David Woodman, Jr.

The Buccaneers of America, John Esquemeling

Incidents of Travel in Yucatan, II, John L. Stephens

A Guide to Historic Galveston, Douglas Zwiener and Elisabeth Darst

Galveston Daily News, June 6, 1937

War of the Rebellion, Official Records, Navies & Armies

Memoirs of an Engineer in the Confederate Army in Texas, Maj. Getulius Kellersberger

Texas Coastal Defense, Alwyn Barr, Southwestern Historical Quarterly XLV

The Official Atlas of the Civil War

Beaumont Enterprize, June 29, 1970, August 29, 1970, September 1, 1970

Legend of the Big Plantation, Francis Norman Wagner

Liberty, Liberty County, and the Atascosito District, Miriam Partlow

Speech delivered to the Harris County Heritage Society, 1971, Ann Wilson

Rice University Review, Vol. 11, No. 1 Spring-Summer 1976

Diary of a Young Man in Houston, 1838, Andrew F. Muir, ed. *Southwestern Historical Quarterly*, LIII

Journal of Lewis Birdsall Harris, 1836-1842, *Southwestern Historical Quarterly* XXV

The Island and City of Galveston, Charles W. Hayes

History of Galveston, Texas, C. E. Griffin

St. Louis' Isle: or, Texiana, Charles Hooten

Map of Texas—1939, J. H. Colton

J. O. Dyer Scrapbook, Rosenberg Library, Galveston, Texas

Ben C. Stuart Scrapbook, Rosenberg Library

Louisiana Historical Quarterly, VII, XX, XI, XXII, XXIII, XXIV

Apostillas, Eduardo Posada

Beaumont Enterprize, April 8, 1934

Here and There in Yucatan, Alice Leplongeon

Gustav Dresel's Houston Journal, Trns. Max Freund

Journal of Jean Laffite, Jn. Laffite

Galveston Island, The Journal of Francis Sheridan, 1839-1840, Willis Pratt, ed.

The Golden Conquistadors, Irwin Blacker and Harry Rosen

Map and Description of Texas, 1840, Francis Moore

Texan Emigrant, Edward Stiff

Evacuation of Texas, Vicente Filisola

Lafitte the Pirate, Lyle Saxon

Texas and The Texas Diary, Mary Austin Holley

The Houston Post, May 24, 1970

The Houston Chronicle, June 10, 1976

The Sword Was Their Passport, Harris Gaylord Warren

Drama and Conflict, The Texas Saga of 1776, Weddle and Thonoff

Life and Select Literary Remains of Sam Houston, William Crane

Handbook of American Indians North of Mexico, Frederick Hodge

Texas As It Was Then, Chris Emmett

Reminiscences, Dilue Harris—*Southwestern Quarterly* Vol. IV

Handbook of Texas, Walter Prescott Webb, ed.

Papers of Mirabeau Buonaparte Lamar

The Day of San Jacinto, Frank X. Tolbert

Houston, Bureau of Research in the Social Sciences of the University of Texas

The War in Texas, Benjamin Lundy

The San Jacinto Campaign, E. C. Barker—*Southwestern Historical Quarterly*, Vol. IV

A Critical Anaylsis of the San Jacinto Campaign—Southwestern Historical Quarterly Vol. LIX

History of Texas, J. H. Brown

The Houston Daily Post, April, 1899

Galveston News, April 11, 1917

The Houston Press, June 12, 1934

The Houston Post, September 19, 1937

The Houston Chronicle, December 12, 1937

The Houston Post, November 23, 1947

The Houston Chronicle, August 19, 1949

The Houston Chronicle, August 26, 1949

The Houston Chronicle, March 21, 1950

The Houston Chronicle, March 9, 1952

The Houston Chronicle, November 17, 1956

The Sunday Enterprize, November 25, 1956

The Houston Press, May 30, 1959

The Houston Post, October 4, 1964

The Houston Post, August 8, 1965

Deed Records and Map Records of Harris County

Deed Records and Map Records of Galveston County

Personal interviews with descendants of Sam Houston, pirates of Jean LaFitte, and early Texas settlers.

Index